Car Ferri

of the Irish Sea

1954–2004

Justin Merrigan

Colourpoint

For Phil – my First Mate
on life's ocean

6 5 4 3 2 1

© Justin Merrigan and Colourpoint Books 2004

Designed by Colourpoint Books, Newtownards
Printed by The Universities Press (Belfast) Ltd

ISBN 1 904242 25 1

Colourpoint Books
Colourpoint House
Jubilee Business Park
21 Jubilee Road
NEWTOWNARDS
County Down
Northern Ireland
BT23 4YH
Tel: 028 9182 0505
Fax: 028 9182 1900
E-mail: info@colourpoint.co.uk
Web-site: www.colourpoint.co.uk

Justin Merrigan was born in Manchester, England, to Irish parents, in 1969 but moved to Ireland three years later. Growing up within the sight and sounds of Dun Laoghaire harbour, the activities surrounding the Holyhead ferries soon became a fascination.

In 1980, at the age of just ten years he was warmly welcomed on board Sealink's *St Columba* by Captain Len Evans; being shown over the ship by the Master created a lasting impression on the youngster. During his school years Dun Laoghaire harbour was his playground, friendly Harbour Constables and Sealink staff nurturing within him a deep interest in the port's link with Holyhead, served by countless British Rail, Sealink and later Stena Line ferries.

In 1987 Justin joined the Commissioners of Irish Lights as an Ordinary Seaman on board the Lighthouse Tender *Atlanta*, a position he enjoyed immensely but which was to be short-lived due to the sale of that ship. Finding secure employment ashore he maintained his involvement with the sea writing for *Sea Breezes*, the highly respected magazine of ships and the sea, covering worldwide ferry operations for that publication for some 13 years. In addition he also served as a member of the crew, and later committee, of the Dun Laoghaire branch of the Royal National Lifeboat Institution.

By 1994 his interest in ferries developed to the point where he embarked on a career in the ferry industry, specifically in port operations at both Dun Laoghaire and Dublin, with Stena Line and the Isle of Man Steam Packet Company respectively.

His subsequent knowledge of the industry led him to accept an opportunity to work at the forefront of the fast ferry industry and in December 1999 he left Ireland for the distant shores of Australia where, along with his wife and four children, he continues to live and work.

Cover photographs:

Front: *Caledonian Princess*   *Stan Basnett*
Superstar Express, Stena Adventurer (II)
both Gary Davies/Maritime Photographic

Rear: Irish Ferries' *Jonathan Swift* speeds across Dublin Bay, with Dalkey beyond, at the start of a late afternoon trip to Holyhead in May 2003.   *Paul Savage*

Frontispiece: British Rail Shipping's *Holyhead Ferry 1.*
     FotoFlite

Contents

Foreword
by Capt Tudor Jones

When Justin asked if I would like to write the foreword to this book, it began to focus my mind on the 50 years being covered, although my family has a further 100 years connection, back to 1853, with packets/ferries operating from Holyhead. A life-saving medal, awarded to my great-great grandfather who was serving as a deck officer on the vessel *Eblana*, is in my possession along with the citation.

As a youngster I grew up seeing all the ships working from Holyhead in the 1950s at very close quarters, as they berthed, and dry-docked, a mere ships length or two from our house near the quayside. Family members sailed in and out just like my Chief Engineer father. So did ships from Fishguard, Heysham, Stranraer and South Coast ports calling at Holyhead for their annual overhauls, with my grandfather working in the marine workshops on those repairs.

Surprise, I also went to sea. Following some ten years of mainly Far East voyages, and obtaining my Master's Certificate, I returned to the port and began sailing on the various ships – cargo, mail steamers and, of course, car ferries, later to be called multi-purpose roll-on roll-off vessels.

Occasional inter-port transfers and dry-dock reliefs would see us operating from the other Irish Sea ports belonging to British Rail Shipping, later Sealink British Ferries, and now Stena Line.

In 1977, the Holyhead route was given a major boost with the introduction of the much larger bow and stern-loading ship *St Columba* and this increased traffic levels to new heights. Apart from the passenger carrying figure of 2400, the task of loading the various vehicles became easier and quicker compared to the older ships, once we had mastered the mezzanine decks and the number to use for each individual loading. She was excellent for the service and a fine ship to handle.

At about the same time as the arrival of *St Columba*, in the late 1970s, a young lad, Justin Merrigan, would visit us whilst alongside in Dun Laoghaire to say hello, take photos and do the occasional voyage across with us to Holyhead and back. He must have been made to feel very welcome by the different crews, as he has maintained very close contact with many, even now from Western Australia, where he appears to have settled well with his family. Having an input into the fast-ferry industry seems to be the perfect career for such an enthusiast.

Large fast ferries and conventional ships are combining to complete the period of 50 years covered by this book, and I have been lucky enough to see at close range the changing shape and enlargement of Holyhead port to accommodate these vessels.

I have no doubt that this book will be of as much interest to the travelling public as it will be to shipping enthusiasts and historians.

Capt Tudor Jones
Retired Master,
Sealink, Holyhead.

Introduction
The development of the Irish Sea car ferry

Commonly known as the Irish Sea, the stretch of water west of mainland Britain, from the northeast coast of Northern Ireland to an area off Cork, actually consists of four individually named areas.

As defined by Admiralty Sailing Directions – Irish Coast Pilot, the true area of the Irish Sea is actually between the east coast of Ireland and west coast of mainland Britain, bounded on the south by a line from the Nose of Howth to Carmel Point in Anglesey (56 miles east) and bounded in the north by a line joining Ballyquintin Point and the Mull of Galloway (29 miles).

The area lying south of the Irish Sea is St George's Channel, bounded on the south by a line joining Carnsore Point and St David's Head (42 miles ESE). Beyond this is the Celtic Sea, an extensive area lying south of Ireland, bounded on the west by Longitude 11°30" west and on the east by the west limits of the Bay of Biscay, English Channel & Bristol Channel. To the north of the Irish Sea is the North Channel, an area bounded by a line joining Fair Head and the Mull of Kintyre (12½ miles ENE).

This then is our subject area, which as the Irish Sea qualification in the title suggests, remains in line with common descriptions when referring to this region of ferry operations.

Irish Sea drive-on/drive-off car ferry services actually commenced on 7 July 1939 when the *Princess Victoria (III)*, Britain's first specially-built stern-loading car ferry entered service for the London Midland & Scottish Railway between Stranraer and Larne. Sadly the benefits of the huge leap in ferry design that she represented were short-lived for she was lost after striking a mine while on war duty in the Humber Estuary just ten months later.

Much has been written about her replacement, a new *Princess Victoria (IV)* which entered service at Stranraer in March 1947. She too went on to meet an untimely end, being lost on passage to Larne on 31 January 1953 when, during a violent storm, a heavy sea breached her half-height stern gates. Suffice to say her loss, along with so much life, shook the ferry community to the core. The Court of Inquiry later declared that as the *Princess Victoria* was, to some degree, experimental it was all the more incumbent upon the owners to keep her design and construction under constant and expert review as experience was gained. Their failure to do so was a contribution to the disaster.

It is in this air that our story begins. The Railway had transferred the Dover train ferry *Hampton Ferry* north to Stranraer to maintain a car ferry service during the summer of 1953 but over the following winter and into early 1954 there was much long and hard thinking on what path to take for the future development of this new concept in cross-channel travel.

Princess Victoria (IV)   *Stephen Cameron collection*

With ever increasing numbers of passengers wishing to take their car with them on holidays the decision to continue was taken and the *Hampton Ferry* again returned north in 1954 and continued to do so each summer until new tonnage finally appeared in December 1961.

Since 1952 the operation of the *Lord Warden*, England's first purpose-built stern loading car ferry, on the Dover–Boulogne service had been a huge success and in 1959 she was joined by the magnificent *Maid of Kent*. Meanwhile communities on both sides of the Irish Sea could only look on as calls for modern drive-on/drive-off facilities increased.

Finally, in 1957, the British Transport Commission took the decision to order a new car ferry for the Stranraer service. The ball was rolling once again and on 16 December 1961 the new *Caledonian Princess* entered service. She was an instant success, showing what could be done for commercial and tourist traffic by good design and organisation. But other Irish Sea routes were slow to follow and for four years the Stranraer–Larne service was to remain the only drive-on/drive-off passenger route on the Irish Sea.

By comparison Rosslare, in the south, was considered to be an antiquated joke. Here there was not even a road out to the ship's berth, merely a foot passage involving a dangerous crossing of railway lines. Cars had to be driven onto flat railway trucks at the mainland end of the pier for the journey out to the ship's side where they were crane loaded onboard, at a rate of about 15 per hour.

Times were changing, and slowly but surely each of the mainstream services were converted to car ferry operation. Holyhead received its first car ferry in 1965, the rival Liverpool service following three years later. The Isle of Man was very quick to follow Stranraer's lead in 1962 but others were painfully late in entering the new era.

The Heysham–Belfast crossing did not provide its first drive-on/drive-off service until 1970 when the passenger steamers *Duke of Lancaster* and *Duke of Argyll* were converted to stern loading car ferries. At Fishguard, where a side loading service had operated since 1964, it was 1972 before the port's first linkspan was built, despite the provision of similar facilities at Rosslare for a new service to France five years previously.

In a number of cases the new car ferries were outdated even as they entered service. The Belfast Steamship Co's *Ulster Prince* and *Ulster Queen* were classic examples of this and under the flag of P&O Ferries their Liverpool route finally closed in 1981.

Only the fittest routes survived and 50 years after the industry picked itself up following the loss of the *Princess Victoria* the Irish Sea boasts some of the finest car ferry tonnage to be found anywhere in the world.

As early as 1992 Irish Sea operators began to embrace the fledgling high speed car ferry, resulting in a number of new services with drastically reduced crossing times when compared with conventional ferries. However in most cases the region's high speed routes are still operated by first and third generation fast craft and have yet to see the benefits of ten years operational experience and constant design enhancements. It is fair to say that early high speed craft have found it difficult to cope with all the Irish Sea has to throw at them, but the larger vessels of the 21st Century are leaps and bounds ahead of their predecessors in terms of ride control and passenger comfort.

While high speed craft were making their presence felt large RoPax ferries arrived on the scene. Having seen the transition from drive-on/drive-off, pure passenger car ferries, to Roll-on/Roll-off (Ro/Ro) ferries capable of accommodating a reasonable amount of freight traffic, the 1990s saw the advent of the RoPax ship. With high freight and relatively limited passenger capacity, coupled with a speed of just over 20 knots, these ships have, in recent years, become the backbone of many Irish Sea routes. On the short Northern Ireland–Scotland link P&O have invested heavily in new RoPax ships while on the Belfast–Liverpool route NorseMerchant Ferries' ships have resurrected the fortunes of the long haul Irish Sea crossing.

High freight with modest passenger capacity is of course not a new concept and the ships of the old Atlantic Steam Navigation Co, later operated by Townsend Thoresen and P&O, offered such a service. The last ship of the line was the handsome *Europic Ferry* (later saddled with the name *European Freighter* in 1992), which offered capacity for 160 passengers and 40 trucks.

Pure Ro/Ro freight ships are outside the boundaries of this title. However, as RoPax vessels are the modern day development of the freight vessel and passenger car ferry we shall include the considerable number of these important ships (with passenger certificates in excess of 200 persons) which have appeared in these waters.

And beyond the RoPax vessel is the cruise ferry, again offering high levels of freight capacity but with full passenger facilities for over 1000 persons. On the Irish Sea, Irish Ferries' incomparable *Ulysses* is currently the ultimate representative of this class of ship with plush accommodation for 1875 passengers and a staggering 4106 metres of vehicle space, equivalent to 1342 cars or 240 articulated trucks. Although with this enormous freight capability in mind perhaps RoCruise would be a better description.

In 2004 Brittany Ferries introduced their new *Pont-Aven* on the Cork–Roscoff service, pushing even further the boundaries of style for which the French company has become renowned with the travelling public.

Ulysses is far removed from the many and varied ferries that have plied these waters over the past 50 years. The names of many ships became well known to the travelling public, often being inextricably linked with the routes on which they operated for very many years. Some ships only appeared on routes for the briefest of times, providing emergency relief or longer overhaul cover for the incumbent vessel. Whatever their role, each ship has had a part to play in the fascinating history and ongoing development of ferry services in these waters

What the next 50 years of Irish Sea ferry travel will bring remains to be seen. Competition today is at its most intense, as much against the airlines as between rival sea carriers. This competition will continue to drive development and the constant quest for that leading edge in comfort and service. Will we see Wing in-ground effect technology whisking passengers and vehicles to Holyhead at speed in excess of 100 knots? Or perhaps we may even see a fixed link. Who knows? But one thing is certain car ferries will continue to play a vital role in the ongoing links, both cultural and developmental, between the island of Ireland, Britain and, of course, the Isle of Man.

This aerial view of the Port of Larne, with *Antrim Princess* and *Free Enterprise IV* on their berths, shows well the facilities on offer in the late 1970s. The Sealink terminal building is just to the left of the ramp beyond *Antrim Princess*. *Author's collection*

Fishguard's new linkspan takes shape in readiness for the long awaited Roll-on/Roll-off service. In preparation for the opening of the linkspan the side loading *Duke of Rothesay* was provided with stern doors during her 1972 dry-docking at Holyhead. As can be seen, they offered little in the way of headroom.

Brian Cleare collection

This aerial view shows well the layout of the port at Holyhead in March 1985. The *St Columba* is making her way through the harbour to the Station Berth while the *St David* is on the Refit Berth, preparing for her short-lived stint on the Dover–Ostend route. To the right of the picture is the container terminal, since re-developed. The *St Columba* is passing the *Rhodri Mawr*, her sister *Brian Boroime* lying astern, under the container cranes. The railway station can be seen to the bottom right.

Author's collection

Opposite: This is Rosslare Harbour in 1973 with the new *Saint Patrick* undergoing berthing trials. The ship is just moving off the side loading car ferry berth for the Fishguard service before moving up to the port's single linkspan, itself dating from 1967. Prior to 1967 cars for shipment drove out to the berth along a single lane road provided at the expense of one of the twin rail lines. Until June 1965 things were a little more primitive. The lack of a road to the berth required cars to be transferred from and to Rosslare Harbour Mainland station by way of flat railway trucks.

Brian Cleare collection

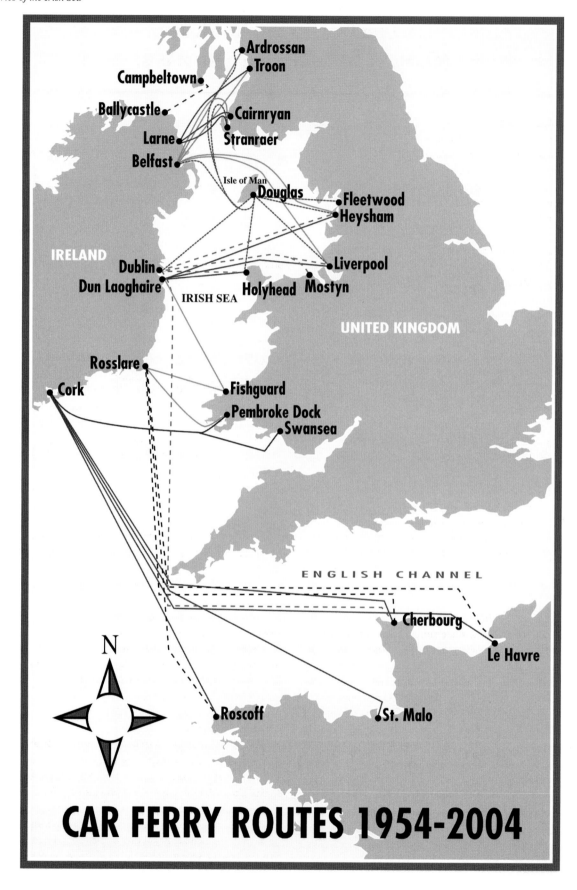

CAR FERRY ROUTES 1954-2004

The Car Ferry Routes
(Dates indicate car ferry operations)

Ballycastle–Campbeltown
Argyll & Antrim Steam Packet Company, 1997–1999

The service between Campbeltown and Ballycastle was launched in June 1997 with Sea Containers establishing the Argyll & Antrim Steam Packet Company, known as the AA Line, to run it. The new company received £8m from public agencies and the Caledonian MacBrayne ferry *Claymore* was purchased and refitted for the service. It was hoped the twice-daily sailings, with a journey time of 2 hours 45 minutes, would create more than 200 jobs and raise £7m for tourism across Scotland.

In February 2000 the AA Line, reporting to be losing £500,000 a year on the route, confirmed it was unable to continue. The final season had operated from June 18 to September 26 1999. Since then various groups have campaigned to have the ferry route re-established, but in 2004 the service appeared to be no closer to reopening.

Ardrossan–Belfast
Burns & Laird, 1965–1971
P&O Ferries Irish Sea Services, 1971–1975

From 1965 the classic *Scottish Coast* of 1956 operated the then seasonal service between Ardrossan and Belfast. To provide for the increasing number of cars on offer the passenger ship was fitted with a temporary ramp and lift in her forward well deck to enable up to 25 cars to be driven on and off.

The next logical step was a purpose built car ferry and the new *Lion* entered service on 3 January 1968, in Storm Force 10 conditions, signalling what was hoped to be better times for Burns & Laird, part of the Coast Lines group. Her arrival saw reductions and eventual closure of the overnight passenger service from Glasgow to Belfast.

Sadly political events in Northern Ireland were taking a turn for the worse and traffic on the route suffered as a result. In an interesting attempt to make the service pay an overnight round trip to Larne was later attempted in addition to her usual Belfast daylight crossing.

In 1971 Coast Lines was taken over by P&O and with it came further hope for the future of the relatively new car ferry operation but by March 1975 the writing was on the wall. Despite the dropping of the Burns & Laird Lines brand in favour of P&O Ferries Irish Sea Services on 1 October 1975, on 12 February 1976 the *Lion* made her last crossing before closing the service and transferring to the English Channel for further service with P&O's Normandy Ferries.

Larne–Troon
P&O Irish Sea, 2003 to date

P&O's response to SeaCat's new Belfast–Troon service was a decision to also offer high speed sailings to the Ayrshire port in addition to the established seasonal Larne–Cairnryan fast craft operation.

Opening the new route on 15 April 2003, the *SuperStar Express* carried a third of the Troon market in her first season. This success was credited to the crossing time of just one hour 50 minutes, 40 minutes faster than the rival SeaCat service from Troon to the centre of Belfast. Following its very successful first season P&O Irish Sea confirmed that the service would recommence on 8 April 2004 for the spring/summer season.

Belfast–Troon
SeaCat (Sea Containers Ferries Scotland), 1999 to date
Managed by the Isle of Man Steam Packet Co since 2003

Launched on 29 April 1999 as an addition to the established Stranraer–Belfast route, SeaCat's services to Troon were an immediate success giving passengers a crossing time of two hours and 30 minutes and a considerable head start on journeys to and from Ayr, Glasgow and Edinburgh, all boasting excellent road and rail connections.

The move was not at all welcomed at Stranraer where sailings were reduced to one round trip daily. It therefore came as no surprise when in 2000 SeaCat announced their intention to consolidate their sailings into Troon with *SeaCat Scotland*.

In 2002 the larger fast craft *Rapide* was introduced onto the run. Later in the year, following the sale of the Isle of Man Steam Packet Co by Sea Containers, management of SeaCat's North Channel operations was contracted to the Manx concern.

In November 2003 SeaCat announced a shorter operating season in a bid to make the service viable. Blame for the reduction was laid at a tenfold increase in the number of people travelling to Scotland with low cost or 'no frills' airlines in the last few years, affecting the viability of the Troon route. The route's season has now been reduced from 10 months a year to eight months.

Stranraer–Belfast
SeaCat (Sea Containers Ferries Scotland), 1992–2000

High Speed car ferry services on the Irish Sea were pioneered by Sea Containers on a new route from Stranraer to Belfast. Making her debut on 1 June 1992 was the new 74m Wave Piercing Catamaran *SeaCat Scotland*.

With a crossing of just 90 minutes on the 46 nautical miles passage the immediate popularity of the new service illustrated that passengers were very keen to experience the new high speed concept. A new day trip market was created and businesspersons using the route benefited from a longer day ashore.

Following the introduction of the Troon service in 1999 sailings to Stranraer were reduced. In 2000 Stranraer was abandoned in favour of a full service to Troon.

Stranraer–Larne
British Railways, 1948–1961
Caledonian Steam Packet Co (Irish Services) Ltd, 1961–1963
British Rail, 1963–1979
Sealink (Scotland) Ltd, 1979–1984
Sealink British Ferries, 1984–1990
Sealink Stena Line, 1990–1993
Stena Sealink Line, 1993–1995

Struggling for survival since the 1953 loss of the *Princess Victoria* the decision to order a replacement vessel for the route was a long time coming and it was not until 5 April 1961 that Wm Denny & Bros at Dumbarton launched the *Caledonian Princess*. The ship could accommodate up to 1400 passengers and 103 cars and was very much a breath of fresh air on the 33 mile crossing.

In the aftermath of the loss of the *Princess Victoria* a measure of the doubts that the owners of the new ship had in the service was the creation of the Caledonian Steam Packet Co (Irish Services) Ltd. This was established by the British Transport Commission to separate the new ship from the rest of the fleet, enabling it to monitor her performance on the route. The implication was clear; if the service was not a success then the *Caledonian Princess* would be transferred elsewhere.

The first year of operation showed an increase in passenger traffic of 20% and in vehicular traffic of 35%. Into 1963 and beyond the figures continued their upward trend. Stranraer's new drive-on/drive-off service was here to stay and in 1965 British Rail, who had taken over management of the route in 1963, ordered the *Antrim Princess*.

Steady growth on the service saw the new *Ailsa Princess* arrive on the North Channel in 1971 and together with the 'Antrim' and various roll-on/roll-off freight ships they maintained an intensive schedule on the crossing, offering by the late 1970s up to 16 sailings a day in peak periods.

Shortly after the formation of Sealink UK, and its subsidiary Sealink Scotland Ltd, a new ship was launched for the Stranraer–Larne service. The arrival of the new generation *Galloway Princess* in 1980 was a real boon for all concerned with the route. The first of a quartet of new ships ordered from Belfast's Harland & Wolff for various Sealink routes, she represented the very latest in car ferry design and went on to serve Stranraer impeccably until her withdrawal in 2002.

On 8 July 1984 Sealink UK Ltd was sold to Bermuda-based Sea Containers for the paltry sum of £66m. Included in the sale were 37 ships, 24 routes and ten ports, including the Stranraer–Larne service and the port of Stranraer itself. Restyled as Sealink British Ferries many new and ambitious plans were announced including replacement of the *Antrim Princess*. Eventually the *St David*, the

fouth and final ship of the Harland & Wolff quartet, arrived on the service, joining the 'Galloway' and *Darnia* but releasing the 'Antrim' for charter to the Isle of Man Steam Packet Company.

Another sale saw the bulk of Sealink British Ferries' operations pass to Sweden's Stena Line on 31 May 1990 for £259m. The company was no stranger to the Irish Sea having chartered many vessels to British Rail and Sealink over the years. Stena wasted no time in announcing their intentions for their new company and on 7 April 1991 the third ship of the Belfast quartet entered service from Larne as the *Stena Antrim*. Formerly the *St Christopher* she was renamed for her new role, along with the majority of the rebranded Sealink Stena Line fleet, to reflect the change of ownership.

By 1995 speculation of a withdrawal from Larne in favour of Belfast began to mount. Despite denials of such plans by a reinvented Stena Sealink Line the rumours failed to go away. The revelation that the second of Stena's revolutionary HSS craft was destined for Stranraer brought the curtain down on Sealink's involvement with Larne and on 11 November 1995 the final Stranraer sailings were operated from the Co Antrim port.

Stranraer–Belfast
Stena Line, 1995 to date

Belfast's second link with Stranraer commenced service from a new terminal, purpose built for Stena, on 12 November 1995. Six weeks later the Sealink brand name was dropped in favour of Stena Line – the takeover process was complete.

The revolutionary HSS *Stena Voyager* entered service between Belfast and Stranraer on 21 July 1996, but her introduction was not plain sailing. Shortly after the inauguration of HSS sailings a revised schedule had to be introduced following problems with passage times. A speed restriction in Belfast Lough on the 40 knot craft brought longer crossing times and severe delays.

Advanced plans to return the conventional ferries to Larne to take advantage of the shorter crossing time came to nothing. However Stena Line's failure to complete the new HSS terminal at the Scottish port continued to prompt fears that the company might transfer the *Stena Voyager* to a new Belfast–Holyhead route. While Belfast enjoyed an ultra-modern facility Stranraer was left with temporary facilities with foot passenger boarding over the craft's vehicle deck.

Finally, on the back of plans to purchase P&O's Liverpool–Dublin and Fleetwood–Larne Ro/Ro freight services, in 2003 Stena Line revealed its intention to transfer their Stranraer operation to a new terminal at Cairnryan to operate alongside P&O Irish Sea's Cairnryan–Larne service. Stena Line will acquire 50% of the P&O port, which will be rebuilt to accommodate Stena Line's HSS and conventional ferry in addition to a new linkspan to serve P&O's operation. At Belfast a new terminal closer to the open sea is also planned. As it happened Stena only managed to acquire P&O's Fleetwood operation, take over of the Liverpool route being blocked by the Competition Commission.

Larne–Cairnryan

Atlantic Steam Navigation Co (European Ferries Group), 1973–1974

Townsend Thoresen (European Ferries Group), 1974–1987

P&O European Ferries, 1987–1998

P&O Irish Sea, 1998 to date

A happy occasion on P&O Irish Sea's Larne–Cairnryan route on 10 July 2003 were the celebrations to mark 30 years of service on the crossing.

Today the Larne–Cairnryan crossing is one of P&O's most successful routes, going from strength to strength, particularly since the withdrawal of Stena Sealink services at Larne. From its humble beginnings of just one ship, the Atlantic Steam Navigation Co's *Ionic Ferry* with a capacity of 30 units and 218 passengers and operating just two round trips per day, the route in 2004 boasts a three-ship operation with a combined capacity of 1620 passengers and 1550 vehicles and a schedule of up to 18 daily crossings.

A full, albeit seasonal, passenger car ferry service was offered by the European Ferries Group under the Townsend Thoresen banner from 1 July 1974 when the1200 passenger *Free Enterprise III* joined the *Ionic Ferry,* which was still primarily a freight ship. Later that year the group purchased the Larne Harbour Company.

Despite a rather shaky start the shortest crossing to Scotland was a considerable success and this followed through the introduction of the larger *Free Enterprise IV* and extension of the full passenger service to year round operation.

In 1996, the record-breaking one-hour high speed crossing was established, a service which has never been matched or beaten.

The year 2000 saw the introduction of two new purpose-built ships, the RoPax vessels *European Causeway* and her sister ship *European Highlander*, both of which offer excellent onboard service with a first-class reliability record.

P&O's port facilities at Cairnryan are earmarked for major development over the next couple of years with the announcement that Stena plan to transfer their Stranraer operation to Cairnryan to operate alongside P&O Irish Sea's Cairnryan–Larne service.

Heysham–Belfast

British Rail, 1970–1975

Seacat (Sea Containers Ferries Scotland), 1999–2002

The historic Heysham–Belfast passenger service was a late starter in offering full drive-on/drive-off car ferry services and while successes at Holyhead and Stranraer multiplied, progress on the direct Northern Ireland–England service was non-existent.

Following the departure of the *Duke of Rothesay* for Fishguard in 1967 the Heysham service was left with her sisters *Duke of Lancaster* and *Duke of Argyll*. In 1969 the news that the route had been waiting for finally came, although the upgrade was by the conversion of the passenger ships to stern loading car ferries and not by ordering purpose-built ships.

On 23 May 1970 HRH Princess Alexandra inaugurated the new service. In 1971 the time honoured overnight schedules continued but daily daylight sailings were only offered between 19 July and 21 September, a somewhat shorter season than that offered the previous year. By 1973 the crossing was in real trouble, the political situation in Northern Ireland having played its part. In an attempt to revive interest in the service First Class facilities were re-introduced, having been dispensed with when the ships were converted, but the rot had set in and talk of closure stalked the crews

Talk became reality and in March 1975 closure of the night service from 7 April was announced. The final sailings actually took place two days earlier with the *Duke of Argyll*'s sailing to Belfast and the *Duke of Lancaster*'s sailing to Heysham.

Passenger sailings between the two ports were resurrected in 1999 when Sea Containers placed the high speed catamaran *Seacat Danmark* on a new seasonal service. The response to the new service was excellent. In particular the new service was welcomed by the tourism industry on both sides of the Irish Sea, recognising the great potential to develop tourism in Northern Ireland at a time when the beautiful province was entering peaceful times. The service also provided excellent access to the England's Lake District, Blackpool and the Lancaster/Morecambe areas, which are all popular destinations for holidaymakers.

The success of the first season prompted the replacement of *SeaCat Danmark* with the larger monohull fast craft *SuperSeaCat Two* in 2000. Technical problems forced a premature closure at the end of the season. The 2001 season brought the *Hoverspeed Great Britain* from the English Channel while 2002 brought the larger *Rapide*. Technical problems again beset the operation and following another premature end to sailings it was announced that the route would not reopen in 2003.

Douglas–Belfast

Isle of Man Steam Packet Co Ltd, 1972 to date

Seasonal car ferry sailings between Douglas and Belfast commenced on 4 July 1972 with the new side loading *Mona's Queen* making the first crossing. Each year since then the Belfast service has remained an important part of the Isle of Man Steam Packet's schedules to and from Ireland. In recent years services to Belfast have been operated by the fast craft *SeaCat Isle of Man*, normally between Easter and the end of September.

Belfast–Liverpool

Belfast Steamship Co, 1967–1971

P&O Ferries, 1971–1981

Belfast Car Ferries, 1982–1990

Norse Irish Ferries, 1992–1999

NorseMerchant Ferries, 1999 to date

The Belfast Steamship Co jumped on the car ferry bandwagon in 1966 with an order for two stern loading ships for the Belfast–Liverpool route. This was the opportunity all connected with the crossing had waited for, as they attempted to cope with the increasing number of passengers wishing to take their cars with them on their travels.

Sadly, as it soon became abundantly clear, it was an opportunity missed. On 19 April 1967 the *Ulster Prince* entered service, followed on 6 June by the *Ulster Queen*. But when British Rail's *Antrim Princess* was introduced at Larne later that year, and following B&I's car ferry inauguration at Dublin with the *Munster* in 1968, serious shortcoming were found in Belfast's new ships.

As stern loaders they were restricted to carrying a worthless amount of freight thanks to insufficient vehicle deck headroom. Overall the design was the result of a complete lack of foresight by the Directors of the Belfast Steamship Co who, it has to be said, were still ensconced in an era of carthorses and crane loading. With the roll-on/roll-off boom about to take off, the new ships were little more than conventional mailboats with a token car capacity.

The Northern Ireland 'Troubles' added to the problems. As we have already seen 1971 saw Coast Lines' operations, including the Belfast Steamship Co, taken over by P&O. Hopes for new ships were high but sadly nothing was to change.

Ten years later the route was still being operated by two ships which were, in reality, outdated when built. The result was predictable. Over the New Year period in January 1981, amidst much industrial strife, P&O announced the closure of the crossing with immediate effect. The ensuing uproar brought a reprieve and on 8 January services resumed, but it was a short-lived effort. By October the route was on course to lose £1m by the end of the year. P&O's action was swift and another closure was announced for 12 October. This was later put back until 11 November as frantic efforts were made by the Unions and Government ministers, all to no avail. The end actually came on 6 November when the *Ulster Queen* failed to leave Liverpool, her crew 'sitting-in' on board the vessel at her Prince's Dock terminal. She was joined the following morning by the *Ulster Prince*, bringing the curtain down on 128 years of services from the Dock to the centre of Belfast.

Just two months later hopes arose when Irish Shipping's Irish Continental Line was linked to media reports that services on the route could resume. An announcement from the company's Dublin head office confirmed that a new subsidiary, Belfast Car Ferries, had been incorporated as a private company in Northern Ireland to open a 'new' route between Belfast and Liverpool

Having been released from Irish Continental Line service at Rosslare the former *Saint Patrick* was transferred to the newly formed company and as the *Saint Colum 1* she reopened the route on 1 May 1982. She very quickly showed, with a decent ship and reasonable freight capacity, how successful the route could have been as traffic figures rose to healthy levels.

However the new operation's one setback was that it was a single ship service. With overnight sailings from Belfast and daylight sailings from Liverpool the *Saint Colum 1* was to say the least, hard worked. Engine troubles in later years often brought the crossing to a standstill at a time when car deck space was at a premium thanks to ever increasing freight traffic.

Towards the end of the 1980s passenger numbers dwindled in face of strong competition from shorter routes and airlines. The one sector to remain constant was freight, but the *Saint Colum 1* was now a victim of her own success and she lacked the necessary space to accommodate further traffic growth. Again the lack of a suitable ship was to sound a death knell and, for the second time, the Belfast–Liverpool service was closed, the final sailing leaving for Liverpool on 14 October 1990.

Convinced that there was indeed a future for a direct service from Northern Ireland to England a group of Northern Irish hauliers and a Scandinavian shipping company combined to launch Norse Irish Ferries in 1992.

In 1997 the company was greatly enhanced by the introduction of the new RoPax vessels *Lagan Viking* and *Mersey Viking*, combining high freight capacity with accommodation for 340 passengers on each ship. Two years later the company was bought by Irish Sea freight operator Merchant Ferries and the two businesses merged to form NorseMerchant Ferries.

After decades of lobbying, in 2002 Liverpool's River Mersey was finally provided with a river berth for Ro/Ro ferries. On 17 June passengers, both private motorists and commercial truck drivers, were welcomed aboard the *Mersey Viking* by Capt Mario Piazza, prior to NorseMerchant Ferries' inaugural sailing from the new Twelve Quays Terminal, opposite Liverpool's famous Pier Head, to Belfast. As vessels no longer had to pass through Liverpool's enclosed dock system, crossing times on the route improved substantially.

However celebrations were short-lived for, not through any fault of its own, the crossing sailed into trouble in January 2003 when parent company Cenargo entered into a Chapter 11 bankruptcy proceeding in the United States. The following month an administrator was appointed, but seeing the strong position of the Belfast–Liverpool route it was business as usual for the Irish Sea operation.

A satisfactory outcome was achieved in September 2003 with a restructuring of the Cenargo group, trading under the NorseMerchant banner with a significantly reduced debt load. No changes have been made to the local management teams in NorseMerchant's flagship business in the Irish Sea, NorseMerchant Ferries, which continues to be run by Phil Shepherd as its Managing Director. Mr. Shepherd summed it up saying:

> NorseMerchant Ferries' trading has not only remained stable but even improved throughout the administration process. I attribute this to the strong support received from a very loyal customer base, and to the incredible co-operation received from creditors, suppliers and staff. It is a testament to their willingness to see a strong business which was over-leveraged survive and grow.

In 2005 the *Mersey Viking* and *Lagan Viking* will be transferred to the Liverpool–Dublin route on the arrival of two new Italian-built ships.

Douglas–Heysham

Manx Line, 1978–1985 (marketed as Sealink (IOM), 1979–1985)
Isle of Man Steam Packet Co, 1985 to date

On 26 August 1978 a ship which was to have far reaching implications for the future of the Isle of Man Steam Packet Company entered service on a new route between Douglas and Heysham. Like a true Viking the new Manx Line's bright and modern looking drive through ferry *Manx Viking* took the island by storm. But her efforts to establish herself were plagued by setback after setback.

Numerous breakdowns and even substantial storm damage to the Douglas linkspan couldn't kill Manx Line's operation, which illustrated just how entrenched the Isle of Man Steam Packet Company had become in their time-honoured way of doing business. Struggling with financial difficulties Manx Line was rescued by British Rail Sealink (60%) and James Fishers of Barrow (40%). Just when the Steam Packet had thought Manx Line was finished the fledgling operation now had the might of Britain's largest ferry company behind it.

The Manx Line operation gradually settled down, taking a large chunk of market share from the Steam Packet. By 1981 the company was being marketed with the Sealink brand name and on 16 April the *Manx Viking* returned to service from overhaul in full Sealink colours, apart from the Manx 'Three Legs of Mann' on her funnels. Sealink had well and truly arrived in Douglas.

From time to time the *Manx Viking* suffered engine problems but in such cases Sealink always found a replacement vessel and services continued to operate with as little inconvenience to passengers as possible. These occasions, and also during overhaul periods, brought numerous interesting 'visitors' to the Isle of Man, each placing an unwelcome spotlight on the Steam Packet's traditional fleet.

Eventually the Steam Packet took the plunge and opted to introduce their first roll-on/roll-off passenger car ferry, purchasing the *Mona's Isle* in October 1984. But it was too little, too late for by now the venerable Isle of Man Steam Packet Company was in deep financial trouble and in very real danger of closing. On the island emotions ran high as tough questions were being asked.

In February 1985 came the news of the intention of the Steam Packet to merge with Sealink Manx Line, then owned by Sea Containers. This caused uproar on the Island where newspaper advertisements pleaded with Islanders to "Support the Merger or lose a 'Packet'". Agreement was finally reached and on 1 April 1985 Sea Containers, through Sealink, became the largest shareholder in the Isle of Man Steam Packet Comppany.

It soon became apparent that the Steam Packet's 'new' *Mona's Isle* was nothing short of an utter disaster for the company and steps were put in place for her disposal after just one season under the Manx flag. In her place came the *Tynwald*, followed in 1990 by the *Channel Entente* (later renamed *King Orry).*

Sea Containers eventually took full control of the Steam Packet and in 1998 the first newbuild ship for the company since the *Lady of Mann* of 1976, entered service. The *Ben-my-Chree*

initially received a somewhat lukewarm reception but she since settled down and proved herself to be a very reliable unit. Following Sea Containers' sale of the Isle of Man Steam Packet Co to Montagu Private Equity Limited for £142 million on 30 June 2003, the company is embracing the future with a level of confidence not seen for many years.

Douglas–Fleetwood
Isle of Man Steam Packet Co Ltd, 1976 to date

The seasonal Douglas–Fleetwood car ferry service opened on 15 June 1976 with the *Mona's Queen*, although the ship was no stranger to the port having called there in 1975 on a passenger-only service. A consequence of the merger with Sealink was the withdrawal of the Fleetwood service at the end the 1985 season. The port's owners, ABP, had other ideas however and during July and August 1986 they chartered the *Mona's Queen* to run midweek 'Funboat' sailings. Since then the Steam Packet, still in association with ABP, has continued to offer an annual link to the Lancashire port.

Douglas–Ardrossan
Isle of Man Steam Packet Company, 1966–1985
Caledonian MacBrayne/Isle of Man Steam Packet Co, 1994–1996

Since the closing years of the 19th century Ardrossan was the terminal for the Isle of Man Steam Packet Co's Scottish sailings. It fell to the *Manx Maid* to take the first car ferry sailing on the route in July 1966, immediately after the crippling national seamans' strike. Over the years each of the company's side loading car ferries operated on the service but by the early 1980s passenger levels had fallen to new lows. On 25 August 1985 the route was closed, the *Mona's Queen* taking the final sailing to the Isle of Man.

An attempt to revitalise holiday traffic between the Island and Scotland was made in 1994 when in association with Caledonian MacBrayne a weekly round trip was introduced using the Scottish company's *Claymore*. The link was again operated during the summers of 1995 and 1996 but sadly passenger numbers simply could not justify continuing and the service was not repeated in 1997.

Douglas–Stranraer
Isle of Man Steam Packet Co Ltd, 1986–1989

The Isle of Man Steam Packet's replacement for the Ardrossan service operated in 1986 to the port of Stranraer, which just happened to be owned by their new partners on the newly merged Isle of Man routes, Sea Containers. The service was a short-lived affair, it being closed on 24 August 1989.

Douglas–Dublin
Isle of Man Steam Packet Co Ltd, 1974 to date

Dublin's historic link with the Isle of Man received its first car ferry sailing on 3 July 1974 when the *Mona's Queen* sailed up the River Liffey. The link is popular with holidaymakers travelling in both directions and who have enjoyed extended seasons in recent years. In addition to the peak summer season, regular Easter, October holiday weekend and Christmas sailings are always well patronised. While the route's mainstay is currently the *SeaCat Isle of Man*, the flagship *Ben-my-Chree* occasionally appears at Christmas, as does the traditional *Lady of Mann*.

Douglas–Holyhead
Isle of Man Government, 1988

A temporary service was operated by the chartered *Bolette* in 1988 when a nationwide seamen's strike looked like hampering the Manx TT motorcycle races. Despite the ending of the strike the service was still offered as contracts with the vessel's owners were final.

Douglas–Liverpool
Isle of Man Steam Packet Co Ltd, 1962 to date

The Isle of Man Steam Packet's core route, prior to the arrival of Sea Containers, offered the company's first drive-on/drive-off car ferry service. The side loading abilities of the *Manx Maid* (1962) and *Ben-my-Chree* (1966) enabled direct loading and discharge at Liverpool's Pier Head terminal, eliminating any possible need to operate into Liverpool's enclosed dock system, which would add up to an hour onto the crossing time.

Following the merger between the Isle of Man Steam Packet and Sealink Manx Line on 1 April 1985 an agreement that the Steam Packet would cease operations from Liverpool, sailing instead to and from the Sea Containers owned port of Heysham, was implemented, in exchange for Sealink undertaking not to operate a ferry service to the Isle of Man. It therefore fell to the *Mona's Queen* to sever the company's historic link with the River Mersey on 30 March.

In 1986 a limited service was reintroduced on the Douglas–Liverpool crossing, a direct result of demands from passengers incensed at losing their city connection. Since then sailings to Liverpool have been steadily increased and on 4 November 2003 a daily conventional ferry service was reinstated with the *Lady of Mann*.

In 2004 a year round service for passengers and cars is available. High speed craft provide twice daily sailings from April to the end of October with a crossing time of two hours 30 minutes, while in winter a service is operated at weekends with the *Lady of Mann* crossing in four hours.

Dublin–Fleetwood
Isle of Man Steam Packet Co Ltd. 1996

Following the peak season in 1996, the Isle of Man Steam Packet operated a trial service between Dublin and Fleetwood utilising the *Lady of Mann*. Despite poor weather, good loadings were recorded, primarily thanks to passengers taking advantage of the service to travel to Blackpool to view the famous Illuminations. The exercise illustrated the potential for using the *Lady of Mann* on non-island traffic and the following year she reopened passenger links between Liverpool and Dublin.

Liverpool–Dublin
B+I Line, 1968–1987
SeaCat (Sea Containers Ferries Scotland), 1997–2003
Isle of Man Steam Packet Co Ltd, 2003 to date
Merchant Ferries, 1998–1999
NorseMerchant Ferries, 1999–2003 and 2004 to date
P&O Irish Sea, 2001

One of the first acts of the Irish Government, following the takeover of the British & Irish Steam Packet Co (B+I Line) from Coast Lines in 1965, was to investigate the introduction of car ferries on their services from Dublin to Liverpool and Cork to Fishguard. Rigorous studies across Europe concluded in 1967 with an order for three ships, two being for the Liverpool run.

Entering service on the new B+I Motorway crossing between Dublin and Liverpool on 15 May 1968, the German-built *Munster* was quite unlike anything else in service in Irish waters, her modern profile presenting quite a contrast with the steam turbine *Holyhead Ferry 1* on the Holyhead–Dun Laoghaire route. Throughout her first peak season the *Munster* made twenty passages per week and during her first eight months of operation she carried 37,500 cars and 175,000 passengers. B+I's first venture in car ferries had been fully justified.

She was followed in 1969 by the *Leinster*, a modified near-sister ship, and together the bow and stern loading vessels offered a new era in travel for Irish Sea passengers. However, being built on the edge of the boom in freight traffic, the ships quickly became outdated and by the mid-1970s they were already capacity constrained. A boost to freight capacity on the service arrived in September 1980 when the two year old *Connacht* was transferred from Cork but although she was joined in July 1981 by a new *Leinster* the company was now in troubled financial waters.

In a bid to better utilise their ships, which until now were spending long periods on the berth between sailings, B+I added sailings on a new and shorter Dublin–Holyhead service from March 1982. The benefits of the Welsh service were all too plain to see and in a battle for survival B&I Line (the plus symbol being replaced by an ampersand as part of a new image in 1986) reluctantly announced at the end of 1987 the closure of the historic Liverpool passenger service. The *Connacht* closed the link on 6 January 1988.

Sealink British Ferries immediately announced a replacement service to Liverpool from Dun Laoghaire but after just 21 months operation this too was closed and Liverpool was left without a passenger link to Dublin Bay.

Some seven years passed before the link was restored using the most unlikely of ships, the Isle of Man Steam Packet's *Lady of Mann*. Marketed as Liverpool–Dublin Direct (under the control of Sea Containers Ferries Scotland), the service was reopened on 12 June 1997 and, thanks to the side loading capabilities of the ship eliminating the need to operate at the former Dublin terminal within Liverpool's enclosed dock system, a crossing time of just six hours 30 minutes made the service most attractive to passengers not wishing to drive to Holyhead. On Wednesdays at the height of the season a high speed service was offered with the *SeaCat Isle of Man* making the crossing in just under four hours. The semi-seasonal route operated until the first week in January when it was suspended for the winter period, but by this time the route was considered a major success and from March 1998 it was operated solely by high speed craft under the SeaCat brand.

The loss of duty free sales in 1999 prompted SeaCat's parent company Sea Containers to consolidate the Liverpool–Dublin service with the Liverpool–Douglas service, resulting in the dropping of the second daily round trip to the Irish port in favour of a Douglas run. In 2003 the service was transferred to full Isle of Man Steam Packet control following the sale of that company by Sea Containers. Under full Manx ownership the future for passenger services from Liverpool's Pier Head to Dublin looks very bright indeed.

While SeaCat's Dublin–Liverpool service was establishing itself competition arrived in the form of Merchant Ferries, a hitherto pure freight operator on the Irish Sea. Introducing the large RoPax vessels onto their new route in 1999 the company ventured into the passenger market for the first time, the *Dawn Merchant* and *Brave Merchant* offering accommodation for 250 passengers in addition to 130 commercial vehicles. Later that year the company became NorseMerchant Ferries but as we have already seen the parent company soon found itself in financial difficulties. The first sign came in 2002 with the replacement of the 'Dawn' with a pure Ro/Ro vessel and a reduction in the passenger service.

On 9 September 2002 NorseMerchant Ferries' Dublin vessels transferred to the new Twelve Quays river terminal on the River Mersey at Birkenhead, opposite Liverpool's Pier Head but shortly afterwards, in February 2003, the *Brave Merchant* was also withdrawn and offered for charter with the Ministry of Defence, passenger operations ceasing entirely. The ship returned to the route towards the end of the year, NorseMerchant Ferries resuming passenger services on the link in 2004. In 2005 two new ships for the Liverpool–Belfast route will replace *Lagan Viking* and *Mersey Viking*, they in turn moving to the Dublin operation.

One consequence of the arrival of Merchant Ferries on the Liverpool–Dublin service was higher levels of competition on the Irish Sea's central corridor, in particular with P&O's freight service on the route. P&O's immediate response was to order a new ship and the RoPax *European Ambassador* entered service

between Liverpool and Dublin on 8 January 2001. The ship was later transferred to the new, and short-lived, Mostyn–Dublin route.

Liverpool–Dun Laoghaire
Sealink British Ferries, 1988–1990

Following hot on the heels of B&I Line's closure of the Liverpool car ferry service was Sealink British Ferries new route from Liverpool to Dun Laoghaire. Commencing service on 25 April 1988, the *Earl William*'s first year on the Irish Sea was a difficult one. Just one week after commencing service all British-crewed ferry services were halted by a National Union of Seamen strike. Sailings did not resume until 15 May but after her false start the 'William' soon settled down. Unfortunately it was not for long and on 11 August the 24 year old ship broke down at Dun Laoghaire. Her morning departure to Liverpool was cancelled and that evening, with two tugs in attendance, she left for drydock in Cardiff. It was two weeks before she returned to service and for the duration all sailings were cancelled with passengers being diverted to Holyhead.

Despite these crippling setbacks the *Earl William* became a very popular addition to the Irish Sea routes. With passenger capacity limited to just 500 and luxury en-suite cabins available for passengers the ship offered a most civilised way to travel. But again she failed, this time on 31 October with generator problems. She struggled on until 4 November when she was withdrawn and all sailings were cancelled. The service reopened five days later when the Portsmouth's *Earl Granville* was pressed into service. By the time the 'William' returned speculation that the Liverpool–Dun Laoghaire route would close was already high.

A reprieve was granted and the Liverpool–Dun Laoghaire service lived to see another year. Still the route operated under a threat of closure and the end finally came on 9 January 1990 when to the sound of a lone piper the *Earl William* left Dun Laoghaire with her final Liverpool sailing.

Mostyn–Dublin
P&O Irish Sea, 2001–2004

The Welsh port of Mostyn joined the ranks of Irish Sea ferry ports when P&O Irish Sea launched a new Dublin run on 19 November 2001. The introduction of the new route was the culmination of a £17m investment which saw not only the development of a purpose-built Ro/Ro terminal and berth at Mostyn, but also extensive dredging.

The introduction of the Mostyn–Dublin service complemented P&O Irish Sea's existing Liverpool–Dublin freight service which continued to operate two freight vessels on a daily basis. Sailing from Mostyn the large new *European Ambassador* reduced Dublin crossing times to six hours, when compared with the longer Liverpool passage.

In May 2002 P&O and Stena announced they had signed a Memorandum of Understanding concerning the Swedish company's proposed acquisition of a significant part of P&O's ferry operations on the Irish Sea. P&O proposed to sell to Stena five vessels and various port assets at Liverpool, Fleetwood and Dublin and to charter to Stena two other vessels, the *European Ambassador* and *European Envoy*. It became obvious that Mostyn did not figure in future plans, "consultations with employee representatives about the possible closure of the service" commencing soon afterwards.

The proposed deal received a setback in November 2003 when the UK's Competition Commission stated the sale would mean less competition and higher prices for freight customers on the Liverpool to Dublin route. Only the sale of the Fleetwood operation was permitted to proceed. P&O retained the Liverpool route but closed the Mostyn operation.

Holyhead–Dublin
B+I Line, 1982–1992
Irish Ferries, 1992 to date
Stena Line, 1996 to date

In a move aimed at better utilisation of their Dublin–Liverpool ferries B+I Line commenced a new service to Holyhead in March 1982. Sailing from Dublin at 1135 and returning from the Welsh port at 1645 allowed one ship to maintain one daylight round trip before making an overnight run to Liverpool. Therefore with two ships, *Connacht* and *Leinster*, a more intensive schedule could be offered serving both routes and reducing the time vessels were lying idle at huge costs.

To say the new route did not get off to the best of starts would be the understatement of the century. News of the new route was greeted with shock by staff at the Sealink-owned port of Holyhead and they vowed to fight any attempt at such a service. At the end of 1981, when B+I made a formal approach to Sealink to use the facilities at Holyhead, the British company took the view that in light of the open ports policy it would not be right to refuse the request and so the Irish company proceeded with its plans.

What followed was without doubt the greatest spectacle ever seen on the Irish Sea. Blockades on both sides of the Irish Sea resulted in a suspension of both B+I and Sealink services on 9 March 1982 and it was not until 4 April that sailings returned to normal and the Irish company established itself on the shorter crossing.

In 1985 once bitter rivals joined forces to rationalise Irish Sea sailings. The partnership between Sealink British Ferries and B+I Line was not an easy or a long one, but it initially saw the *Connacht* serve Holyhead with the British *St Columba* while the *Leinster* concentrated on Liverpool. By the end of 1987, the partnership was finished and the closure of the Liverpool service, after 151 years of continued operation, was announced. The two companies once again went head to head with B&I offering two round trips a day to Holyhead with one ship.

The sale of B&I Line to the Irish Continental Group (ICG) on 1 January 1992 brought much needed investment in tonnage for the company. In readiness for the arrival of the new *Isle of Innisfree (II)* ICG's Irish Ferries brand was extended to the former B&I routes and for the first time the Irish service was able to compete with the former Sealink operation, now under the Stena flag, on a level playing field.

The enormous success of the *Isle of Innisfree* brought even further growth and she was replaced by the larger *Isle of Inishmore* in 1997. Two years later Irish Ferries entered the high speed arena with the introduction of the DublinSwift service but nothing could compare with the arrival of the new behemoth *Ulysses* in March 2001. With this ship we are perhaps looking at the ultimate in size for passenger car ferries. At 50,938 gross tonnes and 10,722 tonnes deadweight she is, in a word, impressive.

While Stena Line's Holyhead–Dun Laoghaire service has always been viewed as the company's premier Irish Sea route, recent years has seen the quiet, yet steady. development of a secondary route to Dublin Port.

Established on 23 November 1995 by the freight only *Stena Traveller*, the new service followed repeated calls for a reduction in Stena Line's freight traffic through the capacity constrained port at Dun Laoghaire. The development of the new HSS service and its associated facilities provided the opportunity for a move and continued further growth in traffic. Complimenting the Dun Laoghaire service the new Holyhead–Dublin route soon built up a steady trade and in September 1996 the link was boosted when the *Stena Traveller* was replaced by sister ship *Stena Challenger*. Unlike the 'Traveller' the former Dover ship was fitted out to accommodate 500 passengers and as such she was a welcome addition proving her worth at times when the HSS was off service. Traffic continued to grow and the 'Challenger' herself was replaced by a larger ship on 24 March 2001, the chartered Italian-flagged *Stena Forwarder* with accommodation for 1000 passengers.

Shortly after the arrival of the *Stena Forwarder* it was announced that a new RoPax vessel with accommodation for up to 1500 passengers, would enter service during the summer of 2003. An obvious response to Irish Ferries new *Ulysses*, the new *Stena Adventurer* is at 211 metres the longest vessel ever to operate on the Holyhead–Dublin route and consequently port facilities at both Dublin and Holyhead had to be extensively modified to accommodate her.

The battle of the giants has begun!

Holyhead–Dun Laoghaire
British Rail, 1965–1979
Sealink UK Ltd, 1979–1984
Sealink British Ferries, 1984–1990
Sealink Stena Line, 1990–1993
Stena Sealink Line, 1993–1995
Stena Line, 1995 to date

The runaway success of the Stranraer–Larne car ferry service led to serious criticism of British Railways and their apparent failure to implement such an operation on the Holyhead–Dun Laoghaire crossing. It must be remembered that the *Lord Warden*, England's first purpose built drive-on drive-off stern loading car ferry, had entered service between Dover and Boulogne as far back as 1952. That the premier Holyhead–Dun Laoghaire service should still be without this technology while cars were being craned onto the mail ships was, to many, quite scandalous!

Endless debates at Government level finally saw progress, but when a new one-class car ferry with accommodation for 155 cars, 1000 passengers and 80 sleeping berths was announced by Mr HC Johnson, Chairman of the London Midland Region, on 9 July 1963 there followed an even greater outcry. At the Irish port the new dedicated berthing facilities for the new ship would force the National Yacht Club to move from its premises near the East Pier! After five months of arguing the Irish Government finally announced that the terminal should be constructed other than at the East Pier. However a temporary terminal was built at the site pending completion of a new facility at St Michael's Wharf in 1969.

The new seasonal service got underway with Dover's *Normannia* on 9 July 1965 and it was not until ten days later that the new *Holyhead Ferry 1* took her bow. Success was instant but despite the introduction of a second car ferry in 1968 it was not until 3 March 1975 that a year round car ferry service was offered, offering one round trip daily (except Sundays), with additional sailings during the summer months.

The arrival of the new purpose-built *St Columba* in April 1977 brought major improvements to the Irish Sea and her ability to accommodate 2400 passengers and 335 cars or up to 35 trucks was impressive for that time. For the next 19 years she maintained the service, joined at times by additional peak period capacity notably in the form of the *Duke of Lancaster*, *Avalon*, *St David* and *Horsa*.

The takeover of Sealink UK by Sea Containers in 1984 brought a rationalisation of sailings in a pooling arrangement with B&I Line. This halted plans for the introduction of the *Prins Philippe*, on charter from Sealink's Belgian partners, and an end to the company's 'second ship' at Holyhead during the summer months. However the tradition was reinstated in 1990 when the *Horsa* joined the route for a season.

By this time the company had changed ownership again and under Stena Line control the *Horsa* was replaced as second ship by the *Stena Cambria*.

In 1993 Stena Line announced that the Holyhead–Dun Laoghaire service would be the first route to receive a revolutionary new gas turbine-powered high speed craft, the High Speed Sea-Service or HSS. Pending delivery of the new vessel the company started fast craft operations with the Incat-built 74m *Stena Sea Lynx* which drastically reduced crossing times from three hours 30 minutes to just 110 minutes. The impact was immediate and rather than taking traffic from the conventional ferries market share grew considerably and one year later the larger 78m craft *Stena Sea Lynx II* entered service.

Delays during the construction of the HSS meant the inauguration of the new craft in time for the 1995 season failed to materialise and it was not until 10 April 1996 that she finally accepted her first fare paying passengers.

With the continued success of the HSS operation, and of what

was originally intended to be a freight-only operation into Dublin Port, one cannot but wonder if the day is not too far away when the routes will be merged into a single terminal on the River Liffey

Heysham–Dun Laoghaire
British Rail, 1970–1971

At a media conference in Dublin on 6 November 1969 British Rail announced that investments in developing Irish Sea traffic amounted to £20m over the previous five years and under 'Sealink', the new brand name for their Shipping and International Services Division, further expansion was the order of the day. A first sign of this was a new service between Dun Laoghaire and Heysham, the company's fifth passenger and car ferry route across the Irish Sea.

The new seasonal service commenced on 27 June 1970, shortly after the fire which severely damaged the Britannia Bridge linking Anglesey with the mainland, resulting in the loss of Holyhead's rail link for over 20 months. Operated until 19 September by the *Holyhead Ferry 1* and *Dover*, in addition to their normal Holyhead sailings, departures were offered on Tuesdays, Thursdays and Saturdays, leaving the Irish port at 0800, arriving in Heysham at 1450 and returning two hours later with an arrival in Dun Laoghaire at 2240. The season was repeated again in 1971 but increasing traffic on the prime Holyhead service brought the end of the new venture and it failed to return in 1972.

Fishguard–Dun Laoghaire
British Rail, 1978

Further cross-pollination was attempted in 1978 when the veteran car ferry *Lord Warden* opened a new link between Fishguard and Dun Laoghaire. With a five hours 30 minutes crossing the service was not a great success and despite initial intentions to run it again during 1979 the route failed to reappear, most likely due to the introduction of the newly acquired *Stena Normandica* on the Rosslare service.

Fishguard–Rosslare
British Rail (Fishguard & Rosslare Railways & Harbours Company), 1964–1979
Sealink UK Ltd, 1979–1984
Sealink British Ferries 1984–1990
Sealink/B&I Line, 1985–1987
Sealink Stena Line, 1990–1993
Stena Sealink Line, 1993–1995
Stena Line, 1995 to date

The Fishguard & Rosslare Railways & Harbours Company was established on 31 July 1894 to provide new harbours at Fishguard and Rosslare, as well as the operation of the necessary rail links with the ships which were to ply the 54 miles crossing. Founded by the Great Western Railway and Ireland's Great Southern Railway, management has been passed through various new concerns over the years but today remains behind Stena Line's operation on the route.

Car traffic on the service began its rapid growth in 1961 when daylight sailings were introduced two days a week during the summer months. By 1963 the situation was quite impossible, the crane loading of cars being tedious and troublesome, forcing British Railways to take action. Their solution was to convert the passenger steamer *St David* to a side loading car ferry in time for the 1964 season.

The improvements certainly helped to offer a better level of service than that of previous years. Some 20,000 cars were shipped on the converted ship in her first season as a car ferry but the route was still very much behind the times when compared with Stranraer and Holyhead. It was not until 1967 that a very real enhancement was made with the introduction of the former Heysham–Belfast steamer *Duke of Rothesay*. She too was converted to a side loading car ferry for her new role but her superior standard of accommodation made her a very welcome addition to the route.

The link finally received a full drive-on/drive-off service on 6 July 1972 when Fishguard's new Ro/Ro ramp was opened for business by the *Caledonian Princess*. Car and freight traffic surged ahead and following the introduction of the larger *Avalon* in 1975 Sealink UK chartered the Swedish-flagged *Stena Normandica* in 1979. The original intention was for her to remain on the link until the arrival of a new building in 1980 but in the event the *St David* was allocated to Holyhead when the 'Normandica' proved to be a considerable success. The chartered ship was later purchased by Sealink British Ferries and renamed *St Brendan*.

Between 1985 and the end of 1987 a rather uneasy pooling arrangement was operated with B&I Line.

In 1990 the route received the splendid *Felicity* as a replacement for the *St Brendan*. For many years the Fishguard–Rosslare service was considered by many to be secondary to the company's Holyhead operation but the *Felicity*, the Irish Sea's largest car ferry, soon dispelled that theory, providing superb accommodation and copious amounts of vehicle deck space freight and cars. The ship remained on the link until 1997 when she was replaced by the *Koningin Beatrix*. She in turn was replaced by the extensively refurbished *Stena Europe* in 2002

Following the success of the high speed 'Sea Lynx' service at Holyhead Stena Sealink Line transferred the *Stena Sea Lynx* to Fishguard in 1994. Fast craft services have remained an important part of Stena Line's services between Fishguard and Rosslare and in 2004 the company purchased the *Stena Lynx III* which had been on charter on the route since 1999.

Rosslare–Pembroke Dock
B+I Line, 1980–1986 and 1988–1992
Irish Ferries, 1992 to date

When B+I Line sought to shorten their long Irish Sea crossings, in an attempt to reduce operating costs, the first route to come under scrutiny was the Cork–Pembroke Dock service, a route itself born out of attempts to shorten journeys. The company turned to Rosslare and on 20 May 1980 the *Connacht* called at

the Co Wexford port for berthing trials. Three days later B+I's chartered *Viking III* opened the new, and considerably shorter, Rosslare–Pembroke route.

Since then the route has had rather mixed fortunes, a plethora of unsuitable ships being used by B+I to compete against Sealink's superior ships. In 1985 a pooling arrangement was adopted by B+I and Sealink British Ferries and this led to the closure of the Pembroke service in January 1986. The partnership between the companies was not a happy one and by the end of the 1987 it was known that both companies would again go their separate ways from the beginning of 1988.

So Pembroke regained its ferry service but again unsuitable ships were used, including the small *Earl Harold* on charter from Sealink. Unable to cater for growing levels of freight the B&I service was quite simply no match for the Fishguard option.

Irish Ferries acquisition of B&I Line for IR£8m in January 1992 changed all of that and one of the first moves taken by the new owners was to charter the former Danish ferry *Niels Klim* for the investment-starved Rosslare service. Entering service as the *Isle of Innisfree (I)* the ship brought much needed freight capacity and for the first time the Irish operation became a very real competitor to the Fishguard run.

With the arrival of the *Isle of Inishmore (II)* on the Holyhead service Irish Ferries transferred their two year old *Isle of Innisfree (II)* to Rosslare in 1997. The introduction of the ship on the southern route had a startling effect on carryings and literally overnight Irish Ferries saw their freight figures rocket. Further expansion came in 2001 when the *Isle of Inishmore* moved south, bringing with her a reputation for reliability and comfort in the poorest of weather conditions.

Cork–Pembroke Dock
B+I Line, 1979–1983

Established on 21 May 1979 when B+I Line withdrew from Swansea in search of greater economies and shorter crossings the Cork–Pembroke Dock service lasted less than four years. With increasing losses B+I Line was forced to look towards even shorter Irish Sea crossings and the Cork service was gradually downgraded until its final closure on 2 February 1983.

Cork–Swansea
B+I Line, 1968–1979
Swansea Cork Ferries, 1987–1988 and 1990 to date

With the introduction of a car ferry service from Cork in May 1969 B+I Line transferred its Welsh terminal from the railway-owned port of Fishguard to a dedicated facility at Swansea. Hopes that a second ship would join the *Innisfallen* on the link failed to materialise. The new *Connacht* replaced the *Innisfallen* on 7 February 1979 but the ship's association with the Welsh port was all too brief, the operation being transferred again on 21 May, this time to Pembroke Dock.

With the closure of the Cork–Swansea passage by B+I Line, followed by the termination of the Irish port's remaining link with

Wales through Pembroke Dock in 1983, working groups in both Swansea and Cork set about trying to find an operator who would reinstate this important link. It was not an easy task and indeed other established ferry companies declined to take up where B+I had left off, primarily due to the long crossing time of around ten hours. With no takers to restart the service local Irish and Welsh authorities took matters into their own hands and decided to do the job themselves. The result was Swansea Cork Ferries and on 13 April 1987 the chartered Polish registered *Celtic Pride* (ex-*Rogalin*) sailed up Cork's River Lee to Ringaskiddy. The Cork–Swansea route was back, albeit on a seasonal basis.

The 1990 season saw the former *Innisfallen (V)* return to Irish waters on charter to Swansea Cork Ferries as the *Ionian Sun*, but trading as the *Celtic Pride II*. A sister of the 1969-built *Innisfallen* the 21 year-old ship was hardly ideal for the route and all concerned were well pleased to see the *Celtic Pride* return in 1991.

Sadly tragedy struck during an August 1992 sailing when two children died in their cabin. An investigation revealed they had been overcome by fumes leaking into their cabin through the en suite toilet, the result of an alteration to the venting system made at some point in her career. It was a terribly sad event, one that shook all involved with Swansea Cork Ferries to the core.

At the end of the year Swansea Cork Ferries was purchased by Strintzis Lines of Greece and the Greek-flagged *Superferry* was introduced onto the run on 5 March 1993. A further sale came early in 2000 and the *Superferry* remained on charter to the new operators for one more season before returning to service in the Aegean. Her chartered replacement in 2001 was none other than the former Irish Ferries vessel *Saint Patrick II*. Under her new name *City of Cork* she fell foul of the safety authorities and was returned to her owners at the end of the season. On 8 April 2002 the *Superferry* returned to the route having been purchased by the company's new owners, Briarstar Ltd.

Rosslare–France (Le Havre/Cherbourg/Roscoff)
Normandy Ferries, 1968–1971
Irish Continental Line, 1973–1986
Irish Ferries, 1986 to date

On 17 May 1968 a new concept in Irish travel arrived at Rosslare with the inauguration of a direct car ferry link with the French port of Le Havre. The route was a joint venture between the Anglo-French operators General Steam Navigation Company (GSNC) and Societe Anonyme de Gerance et d'Armement (SAGA), trading as Normandy Ferries, and Dublin's Irish Shipping Ltd. The Anglo-French operators each contributed a ship, it falling to the French-flagged *Leopard* to open the route.

Two weeks later the *Leopard*'s British-flagged sister, *Dragon*, arrived at the Irish port, but instead of departing for Le Havre she in fact sailed for the Portuguese port of Lisbon. A French national strike had closed Le Havre and it was not until the middle of June before Ireland's direct link with France settled down to offer one round-trip per week.

With 31,000 passengers carried in the first season, 1969 sailings were increased to two per week between mid-June and mid-August. The move paid off and passenger carryings more than doubled to 68,000.

The *Dragon* and *Leopard* continued to operate during the 1970 and 1971 seasons with two sailings per week in peak season. The service was not repeated in 1972, Normandy Ferries permanently requiring both ships on the English Channel.

Under the flag of Irish Continental Line, a subsidiary of Irish Shipping, the route resumed in 1973 using the newbuild *Saint Patrick*. The service began with three return sailings weekly increasing to every second day departures in each direction during the peak summer months.

Four years later in 1977, a decision was taken to expand the service to a two-ship operation and the *Stena Scandinavia* was purchased from Stena Line and renamed *Saint Killian*. One year later increased passenger volumes led to daily services being introduced between April and October and the opening of a second route from Rosslare–Cherbourg.

By 1981 traffic had risen to such levels that capacity was again a problem, resulting in the decision to stretch the *Saint Killian* and purchase a larger ship to replace the *Saint Patrick*. The *Aurella* was purchased from Viking Line and as the *Saint Patrick II* she released the smaller vessel for a new Belfast–Liverpool route in 1982.

The placing of Irish Shipping into liquidation in 1984 was a national tragedy for Ireland. As a subsidiary of the company, Irish Continental Line found itself also under the control of the liquidator. In December 1985 the ferry company was offered for sale but a complex issue regarding ownership of the three ferries delayed any progress for another eleven months. Among interested parties bidding for the company was B+I Line but it was eventually purchased by management and as the Irish Continental Group two new subsidiaries were formed – Irish Ferries plc and Belfast Ferries Ltd.

In 1995, further expansion saw the opening of the new Rosslare–Roscoff route. However a setback to the continued growth of services occurred in 1996 when it was decided to discontinue loss-making winter services to France. Having operated year-round since the service began in 1973, sailings ceased in September to be recommenced in March 1997 and the *Saint Patrick II* was placed on the sale lists. When sailings recommenced they were on a reduced frequency with departures every second day from Rosslare to Le Havre, Cherbourg and Roscoff.

At the end of the 1997 season the *Saint Killian II* was withdrawn from service after 14 years under the Irish flag and subsequently sold. Her replacement in 1998 was the newly acquired *Normandy* which served the routes from Rosslare to Cherbourg and Roscoff. At the conclusion of summer season, operations continued throughout autumn/winter resulting in a return of year-round operations, which continues in 2004.

Cork–France (Le Havre/Cherbourg/Roscoff)
Irish Continental Line, 1983–1986
Irish Ferries, 1986–1997

At a time when Irish Continental Line's Rosslare–France services were enjoying tremendous success the company added a third route to their operations. During the peak months of 1983 the *Saint Killian II* and *Saint Patrick II* offered sailings between Cork and Le Havre in addition to their usual Rosslare services. Cherbourg was soon added to the roster and after the inclusion of Roscoff in 1995 the ships became two of the most hard worked ferries in Europe.

Following a reduction of services at the end of the 1996 season services from Cork were operated on a less intensive basis in 1997. Later that year with the final sailing of the season from Cork to Le Havre, the *Saint Killian II* was withdrawn from service and the company discontinued Cork sailings.

Roscoff–Cork
Brittany Ferries, 1978 to date

Brittany Ferries' weekly seasonal Roscoff–Cork run opened on 27 May 1978 and instantly became a success, traffic levels rising steadily until in 1982 a larger ship was required to replace the *Armorique*.

The *Quiberon* was the mainstay of the service until July 1989 when Brittany Ferries' *Bretagne* sailed into Cork Harbour for the first time, bringing with her a standard of luxury never before seen on any ferry serving an Irish port. In 1993 she was replaced by the even larger, and equally magnificent, *Val de Loire*. Some doubts were expressed by shipping observers as to whether Brittany Ferries could actually fill the ship but they need not have worried, the *Val de Loire*'s reputation for high levels of on board service and excellent French cuisine being an attraction in its own right.

Brittany Ferries' confidence in the future of their sole Irish link has been illustrated by the introduction on their latest vessel in 2004. The *Pont-Aven*, a ship truly deserving of the cruise ferry title, replaced the *Val de Loire* and cuts the crossing time by three hours to 11 hours.

St Malo–Cork
Brittany Ferries, 1993–1996
St Malo Cork Ferries, 1999

A new link to France was opened by Brittany Ferries on 21 June 1993 using none other than the former B&I Line ferry *Connacht*. As the *Duchesse Anne* she operated a weekend round trip from Cork to St Malo, returning to the Irish port in time to take a new mid-week sailing to Roscoff. This pattern was repeated for the remainder of the season and again in 1994. Unfortunately a rationalisation programme at Brittany Ferries saw the closure of the service at the end of the 1996 season.

Another attempt at operating on the route was made in 1999. Managed by Swansea Cork Ferries, St Malo Cork Ferries commenced services, primarily to cater for the needs of Irish livestock farmers. However the service also catered for a limited number of passengers and cars on the chartered Greek ferry *Venus*. The route very quickly joined the ranks of those short-lived affairs of which the Irish Sea has had its fair share.

Dublin–Cherbourg
P&O Irish Sea, 2002–2004

Commencing as a seasonal operation in 2002 P&O Irish Sea operated the only direct sailing between Dublin and France. Using the RoPax vessel *European Ambassador* the Saturday sailing from Dublin proved very popular with not only hauliers but also the travelling public and in 2003 the season was extended by five months, running from March right through until November. Continuing success then led to a further extension to year round operation

The return sailing from France departed Cherbourg at 1500 on Sundays, arriving in Dublin at 0830 on Monday, in plenty of time for her regular Mostyn schedule. The closure of the Mostyn route, together with the sale of the *European Ambassador*, saw the French link discontinued.

The Ships

Built in 1971 for British Rail's Stranraer to Larne service to replace the chartered *Stena Nordica, Ailsa Princess* was a development of the earlier *Antrim Princess*. The ship's maiden voyage between Stranraer and Larne took place on 7 July 1971 and it was to be almost nine years before she operated on any other Sealink service. On 31 May 1980 engine trouble in first *St Columba* and then *Avalon*, resulted in *Ailsa Princess* being dispatched to Holyhead to maintain the Dun Laoghaire run. In 1982 *Ailsa Princess* was transferred to the seasonal English Channel service between Weymouth and Cherbourg, being used as a relief ship during the winter months. She was back at Holyhead on 21 October of that year covering for *St Columba* and *St David*. Following the July 1984 sale of British Rail's Sealink UK business to Sea Containers *Ailsa Princess* was renamed *Earl Harold* (see page 45) for her new owners ill-fated 'Sunliner' service from Weymouth to the Channel Islands. With the regular Sealink Manx Line vessel *Manx Viking* away at distant Falmouth for annual overhaul, the *Ailsa Princess* was relieving her on the Heysham–Douglas run and she is seen at the Number 1 Berth on the Victoria Pier, Douglas, Isle of Man on Sunday 7 February 1982. Through the lens of Richard Danielson she makes a fine sight against the backdrop of the majestic sweep of Douglas Promenade, with its Victorian hotels and guest houses. The linkspan in this view was originally supported on massive buoyancy tanks but after the disastrous events of the night of 1 December 1978, when, in storm force winds and high seas it was torn from its mountings and capsized, it was rebuilt using hydraulic rams with which it was thereafter raised and lowered. The same linkspan remains in regular use today by the Isle of Man Steam Packet's fast ferries.

Richard Danielson

Antrim Princess was notable for being British Rail's first seagoing ship fitted with a bow door. She also broke with the company's long tradition of using steam turbine propulsion for its channel vessels, a move that introduced the funnel design that was to become synonymous with British Rail and later Sealink. The new ship is seen on the Clyde, at Gourock, prior to entering service on British Rail's Stranraer–Larne crossing on 20 December 1967. On 9 December 1983 *Antrim Princess* hit the news headlines when she lost power following an engine room fire shortly after leaving Larne for Stranraer. One hundred and fifty-one passengers and crew were airlifted from the ship which was in danger of running aground on the Irish coast. Thankfully disaster was averted when her remaining crew managed to restore limited power. On 5 October 1985 *Antrim Princess* was transferred to the Isle of Man Steam Packet, following a merger with Sealink, and later renamed *Tynwald* (see page147).

Brian Cleare collection

Built in 1971 for the Danish DA-NO Line and the Oslo to Arhus route as *Terje Vigen*, she was sold to Brittany Ferries in 1975, entering service between Roscoff and Plymouth as *Armorique* on 4 March 1976. Two years later, on 17 March 1978 *Armorique* made her Irish debut at the port of Cork, before entering service on a weekly seasonal Roscoff–Cork run on 27 May. The new link was an immediate success and traffic built steadily until in 1982 a larger ship was required. Later in her career *Armorique* returned to Irish waters on charter to the Irish Continental Group. In November 1989 she operated on Irish Ferries' Rosslare to Cherbourg and Le Havre crossings before transferring to sister company Belfast Ferries to cover the overhaul period of the *Saint Colum I* on the Belfast–Liverpool route. The ship is seen here moving astern onto her berth at Rosslare. In 1993 *Armorique* was back at Rosslare once again maintaining Irish Ferries operations. Later that year Brittany Ferries sold the ship to Xiamen Ocean Shipping Co of Xiamen.

Sean Martley

Seen from the end of Fishguard breakwater *Avalon* meets the full force of a St George's Channel gale. As she points her bows towards Rosslare the ship looks supremely unperturbed. Built as a passenger ship for the Harwich to Hook of Holland service she first ventured into Irish waters in 1968 when she was chartered by Gulf Oil to act as a tender to the VLCC tanker *Universe Ireland* during the opening of the Whiddy Island oil terminal in Bantry Bay. In 1974 the ship was selected as being the most suitable replacement for the *Caledonian Princess* on the Fishguard–Rosslare route, a role for which she was stripped of all her main deck fittings and converted to a stern loading car ferry.
K Barnett, courtesy of Brian Cleare

Through the lens of her Electrical Officer, Roger Paice, the graceful *Avalon* shows her attractive lines, still intact despite her conversion. During her Harwich days the *Avalon* also offered cruises, often sailing as far afield as Stavanger, Vigo and Rønne. Despite being a Fishguard ship, she also spent much of her Irish career at Holyhead. Displaced at Fishguard by the chartered *Stena Normandica* in 1979 *Avalon* officially became a Holyhead ship. Her last Sealink sailing came on 8 September 1980 when she left Dun Laoghaire for Holyhead at the end of her summer season. On 24 September she sailed out of Holyhead for the final time, bound for Barrow and lay-up pending sale. Despite being just 17 years old her thirsty turbine engines made her unattractive to any interested buyers and she was sold for scrap.
Roger Paice

A classic scene as the *Ben-my-Chree (V)* stems the tide when arriving at Liverpool's landing stage in August 1978. This *Ben-my-Chree* was the Isle of Man Steam Packet's second purpose-built car ferry and entered service between Liverpool and Douglas on 12 May 1966. A sister of the *Manx Maid* of 1962, the 'Ben' was built by Cammell Laird at Birkenhead for a grand cost of £1.4m. Unlike other car ferries of the day, *Ben-my-Chree* and her sister were side loading vessels, a spiral ramp linking all decks at the stern and allowing discharge at any state of the tide through a series of shell doors on various levels. The end finally came for the *Ben-My-Chree* at the end of the 1984 summer season, or so it seemed at the time. Having been sold to the New England Development Company for static use in the US, the ship was chartered back to the Steam Packet to assist with traffic during the famous TT motorcycle race period on the Isle of Man. Despite having been laid up for months the old girl performed well during her swansong, running to and from Heysham. Sadly she never made it to the US and after a lengthy lay-up at Birkenhead she was sold for breaking up.

George Danielson

Brittany Ferries' *Benodet* operated the first Roscoff to Cork round trip of the season on 5 May 1984 and is seen here leaving Ringaskiddy dressed overall. The ship went on to become British Channel Island Ferries well-known *Corbiere*.

Jack Phelan

Fred. Olsen Lines' *Bolette* was taken on charter by the Manx Government who were fearful of losing their ferry services to the Isle of Man during the period of the 1988 TT Races due to a seafarers strike. In the event the strike ended but as the Government was committed to the charter the *Bolette* sailed from Holyhead's Salt Island terminal to Douglas between 26 May and 12 June, providing the Welsh port with its first scheduled Isle of Man car ferry route! The ship is seen awaiting an afternoon departure from Holyhead. *Author*

Opposite: The first new build for the Isle of Man Steam Packet Company since 1976, *Ben-my-Chree (VI)* was launched by Mrs Joan Gelling, wife of the Chief Minister of the Isle of Man, at the yard of Van der Giessen in Rotterdam on 4 April 1998. Just three months later, on 6 July, the new ship sailed into Douglas Bay under the command of her Senior Master, Capt Vernon Kinley. The sixth ship to carry that traditional Manx name had arrived home. Sadly Capt Kinley passed away two weeks later and at the time of his funeral many remarked at how fitting it was that he should have anchored his new command for the night in the bay at Port St Mary, just in sight of his house, before continuing to Douglas for the maiden arrival the following morning. Today she provides a reliable and efficient service on the Manx lifeline. In addition to her Heysham sailings *Ben-my-Chree* has also taken the traditional Dublin sailings over the Christmas holidays and is pictured here, under the command of Capt Colin Duggan, swinging in the River Liffey prior to going astern onto the berth in December 1999. In 2001 and 2002 these sailings were operated by the *Lady of Mann*, but the 'Ben' made a welcome return to Dublin during Christmas 2003. In response to growing traffic levels the passenger accommodation on *Ben-my-Chree* was extended during her biennial overhaul in 2004. Carried out by Northwestern Ship Repairers Ltd, Birkenhead, at a cost of £1.5m, the addition of the new accommodation module enables the vessel to carry 200,000 additional passengers annually. *Author*

Merchant Ferries' *Brave Merchant* is seen outward bound from Dublin for Liverpool in August 1998. Withdrawn from the Dublin run in February 2003 the ship was chartered to the Ministry of Defence, followed by Norfolk Line then P&O. A revival in her owner's fortunes saw a return to the Irish Sea seven months later.   *Paddy Cahill*

When Brittany Ferries' *Bretagne* sailed into Cork Harbour from Roscoff in July 1989 she brought with her a standard of luxury never before seen on any ferry serving an Irish port. Big and beautiful, the French-flagged *Bretagne* brought cruise liner standards to the Irish ferry market and boasted accommodation to match; the ship certainly set a benchmark for others to follow. A far cry from the *Armorique*, the introduction of *Bretagne* on the seasonal link further boosted the French company's popularity in Ireland and in 1993 her place was taken by the even larger, and equally magnificent, *Val de Loire*.   *Author's collection*

Caledonian Princess is correctly accredited with being the ship that saved the Stranraer–Larne crossing from closure. She entered service in December 1961 under the flag of the Caledonian Steam Packet Co (Irish Services) Ltd. The new ship was an instant success and by 1964 supplemental tonnage was required to assist with the large volume of traffic on offer. With the route in safe waters ownership of *Caledonian Princess* was officially transferred to the British Railways Board on 1 January 1967. By this time the Caledonian Red Lion Rampant had given way to the black-topped red funnel of British Rail, complete with the white double arrow logo already familiar on other Railway ships since 1964/65. On 26 June 1968 she became the first stern loading car ferry to sail into Douglas, Isle of Man, when she visited with a special day charter from Stranraer. The following month saw her introduction on the Holyhead–Dun Laoghaire seasonal car ferry service, operating alongside *Holyhead Ferry 1* until 5 September. May 1969 saw *Caledonian Princess* join *Duke of Rothesay* on the Fishguard–Rosslare run, side loading doors having been cut into her vehicle deck. The St George's Channel exercise was considered a success and plans were made for a repeat in 1970. For one week in February 1970 the 'Caley P' found herself on the long, passenger-only, Heysham–Belfast overnight crossing but it was back to Fishguard three months later for another successful summer season. In 1971 she officially left Stranraer and become a Fishguard ship. Her reintroduction at the port coincided with the news that from July 1972 a new roll-on/roll-off ramp would be available at the Welsh port, finally bringing to an end the restricted side loading operation in use since 1964. *Brian Cleare collection*

Overleaf, top: The *Caledonian Princess*'s final crossing from Rosslare to Fishguard was on 19 June 1975. After major alterations to her accommodation she returned to the Irish Sea in 1976, operating the Holyhead–Dun Laoghaire route in the company of *Duke of Lancaster*. As it happened this was the final time the *Caledonian Princess* would operate an Irish Sea route and after her final sailing on the last day of February 1977 she returned to the English Channel. By 1981 the ship held the honour of being Dover's final steam turbine ferry and after her last crossing from Boulogne on 26 September she was laid up for sale at Newhaven. Today the ship survives as the *Tuxedo Princess*, a nightclub on the River Tyne at Gateshead – a sad end to a fine Princess, but at least we can be grateful she is still accessible to the public. In this view we see the *Caledonian Princess* steaming out of Dun Laoghaire on her final sailing to Holyhead. *Robert Matheson /Author's collection*

The graceful *Celtic Pride* passes Cobh at the end of a sailing from Swansea. Chartered by the new Swansea Cork Ferries in 1987 *Celtic Pride* was a well-liked addition to Irish ferry services. An added bonus for the new operator came in the form of an extra mid-week return sailing from Cork to the French port of Roscoff on behalf on Brittany Ferries during the peak season. In 1989 a ship could not be secured and the service failed to return. However in 1991 *Celtic Pride* was back, the service having reopened in 1990 with the chartered *Ionian Sun*. In 1992 *Celtic Pride* returned on 6 March for what was to be her final season with Swansea Cork Ferries. On 1 November the ship made her last sailing from Swansea and she was then returned to owners Polferries.   *Jack Phelan*

The *Channel Entente* displays an intermediate Isle of Man Steam Packet Co livery during her first Manx season. Better known as the Dover train ferry *Saint Eloi* the ship was renamed following a relief spell at Holyhead in April 1989 which was, to put it mildly, disastrous. The Isle of Man Steam Packet acquired the ship in February 1990 following trials at Douglas, Heysham, Liverpool, Belfast and Fleetwood. Replacing the *Tynwald,* the *Channel Entente* entered service between Douglas and Heysham on 19 February. With the disastrous *Mona's Isle* still fresh in everyone's memory the *Channel Entente* quickly proved herself to be a reliable and comfortable ship. Her first season complete the ship retired to dry dock at Birkenhead on 27 September and following a £3.5m refit she emerged out onto the River Mersey on 5 December as the *King Orry*. (See also *King Orry*, page 70 and *Saint Eloi*, page 109) *John Hollingworth*

Although she served on the Irish Sea in a freight-only role the French *Chartres* has been included as she is not only a passenger car ferry but also because she is such an interesting ship. The Dover Strait vessel, built as a multi-purpose train ferry in 1974 for winter services from Dunkerque and peak season car ferry sailings from Calais, found herself on the Holyhead–Dun Laoghaire service during November 1992 in lieu of the *Stena Cambria*.
Author

As part of sweeping changes announced by P&O in October 2004, *SuperStar Express* was returned to her owners following her successful Irish Sea charter. Taking her place on the Larne–Cairnryan/Troon run is the Incat-built *Cherbourg Express*, transferred from the Portsmouth–Cherbourg run. *Cherbourg Express* is expected to take up her North Channel duties in spring 2005.   *Gary Davies/Maritime Photographic*

The former *Saint Patrick II* (see page 112) made a return to once familiar waters in 2001 as *City of Cork* on sub-charter to Swansea Cork Ferries, by then under new ownership. In 1989 the ship was chartered to Greek operator HML for their Brindisi–Patras route as *Egnatia II*. During 2000 she operated for BalearExpress between Mallorca and Sete. As the *City of Cork* she suffered numerous problems with safety authorities on both sides of the Irish Sea resulting in cancellations and delays, before eventually settling down into regular service. However the damage was done and after just one season, the *City of Cork* was replaced for 2002 with the returning *Superferry*, purchased by Swansea Cork Ferries from her former owner, Strintzis Lines. The charter of *Egnatia II* by HML concluded during 2002 and, in accordance with the terms of that agreement, ownership of the ship transferred to the charterers who promptly sold her for further trading in Canada with CTMA as the *CTMA Vacancier*.

Paddy Cahill

Probably one of the most unlikely ferries to see service outside the confines of the trade for which she was designed was the *Claymore*, built for Caledonian MacBrayne's Outer Isles services from Oban in 1978. The ship ventured into the Irish Sea in 1994 when she was used during the summer months to operate Saturday sailings from Ardrossan to Douglas in association with the Isle of Man Steam Packet. Unfortunately the venture was not a huge success and was not continued beyond 1996. In June 1996 the ship was chartered to act as a tender between Dun Laoghaire Harbour and the visiting US Navy aircraft carrier USS *John F Kennedy* at anchor in Dublin Bay. In May 1997 CalMac sold the *Claymore* to the Sea Containers subsidiary Argyll and Antrim Steam Packet Co for a new service between Campbeltown and Ballycastle. This seasonal service was withdrawn in February 2000 when the company decided that it was not economically viable. After a prolonged period laid up at Birkenhead the *Claymore* was sold for further trading with Pentland Ferries, for service to Orkney.   *Author*

With the *Stena Lynx* committed to English Channel operation during the summer of 1996 Stena Line chartered her Condor Ferries sister *Condor 10* to maintain high speed services on the Fishguard–Rosslare route.

Brian Cleare

Built by B+I Line to replace the *Innisfallen* on the Cork–Swansea crossing, the *Connacht* was the largest ferry to fly the Irish flag at that time. Her maiden voyage from Cork to Swansea took place on 7 February 1979. Displaying the colour scheme adopted after a major refit in spring 1986, the restyled B&I Line's *Connacht* arrives in Dublin at the end an early morning sailing from Holyhead in April 1988. The refit cost in the region of IR£3m and involved stripping her two passenger decks, removing the majority of her cabins and fitting a new restaurant, buffet, recliner lounge, cinema, bar and duty-free shop. Having closed the Dublin–Liverpool service on 6 January 1988 *Connacht* was transferred south to Rosslare to reopen the Pembroke Dock route six days later. She was later brought back to the central corridor to relieve the *Leinster* for overhaul. This was her final spell on the Holyhead service and she saw out the summer season at Rosslare before her sale to Brittany Ferries in October. (See also *Duchesse Anne*, page 38)

Author's collection

Brittany Ferries introduced the *Cornouailles* onto the Roscoff–Cork service on 31 March 1979 in advance of the main season which was operated by the *Armorique*. With accommodation for up to 500 passengers the ship was seen as an ideal replacement for the smaller 250 passenger *Penn-ar-Bed* on the quieter autumn season sailings prior to the winter closure. In 1980 the *Cornouailles* again opened the season prior to the *Armorique* arriving for the peak sailings. It was to be another seven years before the *Cornouailles* returned to Cork, arriving from Roscoff on 23 March 1987. By this time the ship was painted in the livery of Brittany Ferries' freight division Truckline. (See also *Havelet*, page 57)

Gary Davies/Maritime Photographic

British Rail Sealink acquired *Darnia* for the Stranraer to Larne service in 1977. Formerly the *Stena Topper* she sailed for the Irish Sea and the Belfast yard of Harland & Wolff for a major refit prior to entering service on the North Channel on 10 August 1978. As a freight carrier she offered accommodation for just 75 passengers. The ship is included in this title as she was later converted to carry up to 412 passengers. With the removal of the *Ailsa Princess* to the English Channel in 1982, *Darnia* underwent a major refit to raise her passenger capacity, additional superstructure being fitted immediately forward of the funnel as seen in this view off the mouth of Loch Ryan in March 1986. To call the ship 'tender' after this conversion would be rather kind and she gained a reputation for being able to roll on wet grass. *Darnia* rarely operated away from Stranraer. However in May 1988 she briefly operated on the Fishguard–Rosslare route. In January 1990 she attempted to provide cover for the fire damaged *St Columba* on the Holyhead–Dun Laoghaire service but in the event, she made only two round trips over a five-day period due to gales and she was dispatched back to Scotland. Later that year she was sold by Sealink's new owners, Stena Line, to Nordström & Thulin. Despite her post-conversion reputation for being a lively sea ship *Darnia* served the Stranraer service well and was instrumental in building high levels of all important freight traffic.

Author

Merchant Ferries' *Dawn Merchant* on Dublin's River Liffey. Withdrawn from the service by Norse Merchant Ferries in April 2002 the ship sails today between Dover and Dunkerque on charter to Norfolk Line.

Author

Hoverspeed's Dover-based *Diamant* operated briefly on the Isle of Man Steam Packet's Douglas–Liverpool/Dublin routes in March 2003.

Gary Davies/Maritime Photographic

Entering service on 24 June 1965 on British Rail's Dover–Boulogne service the *Dover* spent a good deal of her career on the Irish Sea, primarily on the Holyhead–Dun Laoghaire service. Released from Dover by the new *Vortigern* on 31 July 1969 the *Dover* sailed immediately to Holyhead to join her near sister, the *Holyhead Ferry 1*, on the seasonal car ferry service to Dun Laoghaire. The partnership between the two sisters was a success, particularly as the *Dover* boasted a larger car capacity, and in 1970 she once again ran from Holyhead for the duration of the summer season. As an experiment from 27 June to 19 September both ships also offered sailings from Dun Laoghaire to Heysham. With a crossing time of six hours and 50 minutes a total of three round trips a week were operated but it was not a success and at the end of the 1971 season it was decided not to repeat it in 1972. (See also *Earl Siward*, page 47)

Nigel Thorntonn collection

The *Dover*, by now ten years old, is seen at the new Ro/Ro linkspan at Dun Laoghaire's Carlisle Pier in 1975. The mail boat *Hibernia* is just visible to the right on the traditional departure berth.

Jim Ashby

In 1969 capacity on the Rosslare–Le Havre service was doubled when the *Dragon* joined sister ship *Leopard*. The *Dragon* was one of the largest car ferries of the day and her accommodation for 850 passengers, was second to none. Sleeping facilities were available for 429 passengers, 276 being in comfortable cabins. On the vehicle deck space was available for up to 250 cars. Ireland's first direct ferry link with France operated successfully for four seasons. However, when the *Dragon* left Rosslare on her final sailing of the 1971 season it was with the knowledge that she would not be back, it being announced that the service would not reopen in 1972. It was to be almost 15 years before she returned to Irish waters taking over Townsend Thoresen's Larne–Cairnryan service as the *Ionic Ferry* (see page 63). The *Dragon* is seen here, from the decks of the *Saint Killian* (her eventual successor on the Irish run) at Le Havre on 30 December 1978. Note the Christmas tree on her main mast!

Jack Phelan

The former pride of the Sealink fleet, the Hook of Holland–Harwich ferry *Prinses Beatrix*, was sold to Brittany Ferries for the Caen–Portsmouth route in 1985, later being renamed *Duc de Normandie*. She has so far only visited Cork on one occasion, that being with the Roscoff sailing on 28 March 1992 following storm damage to the *Havelet*.   *Jack Phelan*

The Heysham–Belfast passenger service was converted to car ferry operation in 1970 with the conversion of the 1956-built *Duke of Argyll* and her sister *Duke of Lancaster* to stern loading car ferries by their builder, Harland & Wolff. The 'Argyll' opened the new car ferry service with the overnight sailing from Heysham on 24 February. In her new guise the ship offered space on her 2m clear height vehicle deck for 105 cars, although just inside the stern door there was space on the centre line for two coaches. Up top, gone was the traditional two-class accommodation for 1800 passengers, one-class facilities for 1400 passengers now being the order of the day. However the route was to close on 5 April 1975, the *Duke of Argyll* taking the final westbound sailing. It was then to Holyhead, as reserve vessel, for her final Sealink summer and under a cloud of belching black smoke the 'Old Duke' glides through the yachts in Dun Laoghaire Harbour. Finishing at Holyhead in September 1975 she sailed to Barrow for lay-up pending sale. Following sale to Cynthia Navigation Ltd of Piræus she left the Irish Sea on 19 October. For almost 20 years the ship enjoyed her further career in warmer climes but was sadly gutted by fire while at anchor off Hong Kong in 1995.

Robert Matheson/Author's collection

Opposite: As the *Duchesse Anne* the former B&I Line ferry *Connacht* (see page 34) made a welcome return to Irish waters under the flag of new owners Brittany Ferries on 20 June 1993. Berthing within sight of her builders, Brittany Ferries marked the occasion in style by hosting a reception on board to which they invited her former B&I Master, Capt Seamus Sydenham and her designer Mr Patrick Martin. The following day she opened the new Cork–St Malo route, returning to the Irish port in time to take a new mid-week sailing to Roscoff. Prior to entering service with Brittany Ferries in time for the 1989 season she underwent a major refit during which most of her original cabins, removed during her major refit of 1986, were reinstated. The *Duchesse Anne* is seen at St Malo during the summer of 1996, her final season before the closure of the Cork link. In October she was sold to Jadrolinija for service between Croatia and Italy as the *Dubrovnik*.

Author

A smart looking *Duke of Lancaster* going astern into Dun Laoghaire. Like her sister, the 'Lancaster' was also surplus to requirements after the demise of the Heysham service – but not for long. The conversion of the *Avalon* to a stern-loading car ferry for Irish Sea service was delayed and so the *Duke of Lancaster* was pressed into service at Fishguard on 19 June 1975. Four weeks later she was released by the newcomer to replace the *Duke of Rothesay* on the summer roster at Holyhead, opposite the *Dover*.   *Robert Matheson/Author's collection*

Opposite top: Once the mailboats *Hibernia* and *Cambria* were withdrawn from the Holyhead–Dun Laoghaire crossing, the Welsh port's 'arrivals berth' at the head of the east side of the inner harbour became obsolete, the traditional 'departure berth' on the west side being fitted with a linkspan for the new multi-purpose *St Columba*. This most unusual view reveals the *Duke of Lancaster* resting on the disused berth in July 1977 having arrived from Dun Laoghaire at 1545hrs to find the *St Columba* (just visible, right) still occupying the linkspan. The larger ship was suffering some engine trouble and it wasn't until 1645hrs that she finally got away some 90 minutes late thereby allowing the 'Lancaster' to move across. As far as I am aware this was one of the last times an incoming ship with passengers used the 'arrivals berth'. Covering for a broken down *St Columba* the 'Lancaster's' final commercial sailing was the morning departure from Dun Laoghaire on 9 November 1978. Under a trademark cloud of black smoke she left Holyhead for the final time on 17 January 1979 bound for lay-up at Barrow. Five months later came the announcement that the 'Lancaster' had been sold to a Liverpool-based company, Empirewise Ltd, for use as a leisure centre on the banks of the River Dee. On 10 August 1979, the *Duke of Lancaster* arrived at her final resting place, a mere 75 miles from Holyhead.   *Ian Scott-Taylor*

Left: Still bearing the her proud name, the *Duke of Lancaster* sits quietly rusting away at her landlocked berth at Llanerch-y-Mor, near the port of Mostyn on the North Wales coast. My last visit to the ship was on 12 September 2003 and what a sad sight she presented. This picture tells the whole story of her imprisonment. Encased in concrete she won't be going anywhere fast and indeed she has now been in this location for longer than her entire seagoing career. Back in 1979 her new owners had all sorts of grand plans for their ship, including a 300-bed hotel with casino, and other leisure facilities. Sadly, it seems she failed to pass planning and safety regulations and as far as I can ascertain she served as little more than a unique venue for a market, her car deck being used for traders' stalls. *Author*

For the Fishguard–Rosslare service the former Heysham passenger steamer *Duke of Rothesay* was converted to a side-loading car ferry by Cammell Laird in 1967. The conversion involved stripping the main deck of all accommodation leaving just the centre casings for machinery purposes. Access for up to 112 average size cars was provided through side doors port and starboard aft. Passenger capacity was reduced from 1800 to 1400 in one class. On completion of the conversion the ship went on charter to the Fishguard & Rosslare Railways and Harbours Company and her arrival at the Welsh port signalled the end of the prewar steamer *St Andrew*. The *Duke of Rothesay*'s first season on St George's Channel was considered a huge success. Returning to Heysham for the winter period the 'Rothesay' was confirmed for another summer in Fishguard in 1968 and by 1969 she was the route's mainstay. In these three views, captured by David Owen on 15 August 1969, the *Duke of Rothesay* rolls her way out of Fishguard into the teeth of an Irish Sea gale. By 1971 it was known that the *Caledonian Princess* would be Fishguard's main ship and the *Duke of Rothesay* was downgraded to relief and summer peak work.   *David Owen/Brian Cleare collection*

With her blue hull paint raised a deck to make way for the new brand name Sealink, the *Duke of Rothesay* steams into Dun Laoghaire in 1973. The ship began the year at Holyhead operating to Dun Laoghaire, then moving to the Heysham–Belfast run before sailing back to Holyhead for further relief duties from March. The ship even got as far as Dover in June but only for one week after which she returned to Holyhead. August saw her back at Fishguard when the *Caledonian Princess* required emergency attention. In her relief role the 'Rothesay' spent most of her time between Holyhead and Heysham but her days were numbered. Replaced by the *Duke of Lancaster* at Holyhead in July 1975 the old girl was sold for scrap. She departed Holyhead, under tow, in October bound for Faslane and the breaker's torch. *Author's collection*

Sealink's Channel Islands ferry *Earl Godwin* served on the Irish Sea on just one occasion. The ship was called upon to relieve on the Douglas–Heysham service between 25 March and 8 April 1981 while the *Manx Viking* was overhauled and repainted in Sealink livery at Holyhead. Today the former 'Godwin' is in Italian service with Moby Line as the *Moby Baby* running between Portoferraio and Piombino.

Stan Basnett

Alongside at Dun Laoghaire is Sealink British Ferries' *Earl Granville*. The ship made her Irish Sea debut when she took up the Liverpool service in place of the mechanically troubled *Earl William* on 4 November 1988. Although she boasted similar accommodation to the 'William', the result of a major 1985 refit on both ships, the 'Granville' was not a success on the 120 mile crossing. Her sea-keeping abilities were notorious, a shortcoming not helped during her two weeks on the run when the Irish Sea was at its worst. The ship ventured back into the Irish Sea in March 1990 for another unsuccessful spell, this time relieving on the Stranraer–Larne service during the overhauls of *Galloway Princess* and *Darnia*.

Author

The former *Ailsa Princess* (see page 23) was renamed *Earl Harold* in 1985. After heavy losses on the Channel Islands services the ship found herself back on the Irish Sea as relief ship. Having covered at Holyhead for the freight ship *Stena Sailer* the 'Harold' was then placed on the passenger service for three days from 11 February 1988 while *St Columba* underwent an engine repair. This complete it was then back to her old stomping ground on the North Channel. April 1988 saw *Earl Harold* on the Fishguard–Rosslare service in place of *St Brendan* which had been withdrawn due to engine problems. Seen from the end of Rosslare Pier the 'Harold' is just about to commence her swing before running astern onto the berth. More engine problems with the 'Brendan' brought *Earl Harold* back to Fishguard in October 1988.   *Brian Cleare*

A very different looking *Earl Harold* is seen alongside at Rosslare in April 1989. The ship was taken on a six month charter by Sealink's competitors B&I Line to maintain the service to Pembroke Dock following the sale of the *Connacht* the pervious year. Generally this was a horrid time for B&I and the charter of the 'Harold' illustrated just how bad things really were. In October she was replaced by another chartered, albeit larger ship, the Faeroese *Norröna*. So the former Stranraer ship's last Irish Sea service was under the flag of Sealink's main competitor, with Nassau as port of registry. The ship was quickly sold and, after further changes of ownership, remains in service in 2004 with Greek operator Hellas Ferries as the *Express Adonis*.   *Author's collection*

Having been converted to drive through operations, and her vehicle capacity increased for Dover Strait services, the former *Holyhead Ferry 1* (see page 58) only saw one more stint on the Irish Sea before her sale in 1981. As the *Earl Leofric* Holyhead's first dedicated car ferry returned to her old route to release the *St Columba* for overhaul in February 1978. I can recall being so disappointed at seeing the turbine's funnel peeping over the top of St Michael's Pier, depriving me of what was to be my first sailing in the 'new' *St Columba*. I may have been only eight years old, but I can clearly remember everything about my passage in the ship, from boarding via her stern door onto the vehicle deck, to her wrap around outside deck affording the best of views, even to the peculiar noises she made as she turned off Holyhead's Mail Pier to run astern onto the berth. Just days before our trip the *Earl Leofric* had damaged her new bow visor at the Irish port following a particularly nasty crossing from Holyhead and so for a large part of her time back on the link she operated as a stern loader, just as she had since her delivery in 1965. Replaced at Dover in October 1980 by the new *St Anselm*, herself later to become Holyhead's *Stena Cambria*, the *Earl Leofric* was sold to Spanish ship breakers. After an amazingly short 16 years she was consider too expensive to operate due to her thirsty steam turbines, and too small in the age of double decked Ro/Ro ships. The ship left Newhaven under tow on her one-way passage on 30 May 1981. I am now glad of that sailing in February 1978!

Jim Ashby

On 19 April 1988, the *Earl William* runs astern onto Dun Laoghaire's No 4 berth for the first time, with a freight sailing from Holyhead, following a fire on board the relief ferry *St David*. Six days later, under of the command of Capt John Davies, she inaugurated Sealink British Ferries' new Liverpool–Dun Laoghaire passenger and car ferry service. During the 1989 summer season confirmation that the service would be closed was received and at 1030 on 9 January 1990 the *Earl William* left Dun Laoghaire for Liverpool for the last time, under the command of Capt Simon Townsend. After destoring in Liverpool she sailed for lay-up at Milford Haven. The *Earl William* made a somewhat surprising return to service on the Irish Sea three weeks later when she was chartered by Belfast Ferries to cover Liverpool–Belfast sailings while their *Saint Colum 1* was overhauled at Birkenhead, but on 9 March it was back to lay-up at Milford. However an even greater surprise came on 4 February 1991 when the *Earl William*, now owned by Sealink Stena Line, was pressed into service on the Holyhead–Dun Laoghaire service when the *Stena Cambria* suffered grounding damage at the Welsh port. The old girl was in a sorry state, her rust streaked hull devoid of company markings and handling affected thanks to a faulty bow thrust unit. The 'Cambria' returned two weeks later allowing the *Earl William* to return to hibernation in South Wales. Sealink Stena Line brought the *Earl William* out of lay-up one more time for a final spell of Irish Sea service at the height of the 1991 summer season. With the *Stena Cambria* delayed during relief service at Dover the *Earl William* was given a much needed face-lift before taking up service between Holyhead and Dun Laoghaire on 29 June. Just over nine months later she was sold for further trade and has since then steadily declined with long periods laid up in a variety of ports.   *Author*

Opposite: Like her half sister, under her new incarnation the former *Dover* (see pages 36 and 37) would also see just one more spell on the Irish Sea. As the *Earl Siward* the ship returned to the Holyhead–Dun Laoghaire service to operate the additional 'second ship' summer sailings from 22 June 1981. The ship operated for just 17 days before being replaced by the chartered *Prinsessan Desirée*. When the *Earl Siward* quietly departed Dun Laoghaire under a cloud of black smoke on 8 July the few onlookers on the piers were not just witnessing the ship's final departure, but the end of an era as the last Railway-owned turbine steamer to operate on the Irish Sea disappeared over the horizon. Four months later she was sold to Sol Ferries of Cyprus for further service as the *Sol Express*. Today, renamed *Tuxedo Royale*, the ship survives as a floating nightclub in a rather depressed area of Middlesborough.   *Nigel Thorntonn collection*

Above: The chartered Italian ferry *Espresso Olbia* heads upstream to Cork's Tivoli terminal on a B+I Line sailing from Pembroke Dock while on a brief charter to cover the *Connacht*'s annual dry-docking during February 1980.

Jack Phelan

Left: The second ship in a new breed of ferry for P&O's Irish Sea services, the *European Ambassador* is a somewhat larger half sister to the North Channel's *European Causeway* and *European Highlander*. Under the command of Capt Nick Spencer the ship left builders Mitsubishi Heavy Industries, Shimonoseki, Japan on 13 December 2000 and arrived in Dublin 25 days later. Having entered service between Liverpool and Dublin on 8 January 2001 the ship was transferred to the new Mostyn–Dublin run 11 months later. Between April and November 2002 she added a weekend run from Dublin to Cherbourg to her schedules, a successful move which was repeated in 2003. Comfortable accommodation is provided for 405 passengers with beds for 222 passengers in a range of two and four berth cabins. A planned takeover of P&O's Liverpool service by Stena Line failed to materialise and the *European Ambassador* was instead sold to the Swedish company and the Mostyn service closed. Dublin's link with France was also terminated.

Ian Collard

P&O Irish Sea's *European Causeway* became the company's first new build for the Cairnryan–Larne service. Entering service on 14 August 2000 the Mitsubishi-built ship replaced the *Pride of Rathlin* and brought the route into the 21st century. Under the command of Capt Jim McMullen the *European Causeway* completed her delivery voyage from Japan in an impressive three weeks. In fact, during her trials, for 15 hours she maintained a steady 26 knots at full ahead. The lead vessel of three similar ships, the *European Causeway* illustrates the now popular RoPax concept of a vessel with high vehicle capacity and relatively low passenger accommodation. The 'Causeway' accommodates 410 passengers and 375 cars or 107 x 13.5m freight units.   *Trevor Kidd*

The Ro-Ro vessel *European Gateway* first appeared on Townsend Thoresen's Larne–Cairnryan service on 17 March 1980. Primarily a freight ship she also offered accommodation for 132 passengers. During her brief spell on the route, covering for the overhaul periods of *Free Enterprise IV* and freight vessel *Doric Ferry*, she became instantly popular and it came as no surprise when it was later announced that she would be permanently transferred to the link early in 1981. For her new role the *European Gateway* was lengthened by 15.7 metres and her passenger capacity was increased to 326. Operating alongside the *Free Enterprise IV* the ship was a major success but tragedy was to strike. In December 1982, while providing overhaul cover on the North Sea, she was in collision with the Sealink ferry *Speedlink Vanguard* off Felixstowe. The ship sank with the loss of six persons. Having been salvaged the ship was rebuilt for service in the Mediterranean.   *Author's collection*

The *European Highlander* left Mitsubishi's Shimonoseki yard on 1 June 2002 and entered service between Larne and Cairnryan on 3 July. The ship differs slightly from the *European Causeway* in that she is slightly longer to allow a second lift and a few extra freight units to be carried. For the eagle eyed observer 'Highlander' also has two extra lifeboats instead of a marine evacuation system.

Trevor Kidd

To operate B+I Line's ailing Cork–Pembroke Dock route for the summer of 1983 came the attractive *Fennia* on charter from Finland's Silja Line. The 12 week operation was a last attempt to make the service work but even with a grant from the Irish Government it failed to pay its way. On her maiden commercial voyage the ship is seen gliding through calm waters passing Roches Point at the entrance to Cork Harbour on 16 June. Perhaps B+I's directors thought that this most challenging of ferry routes was always graced with such kind weather, for while they secured a very well appointed ship she lacked stabilisers and towards the end of the season she gained a reputation for being somewhat lively. Sold in 2001 to the Finnish RG Line, and renamed *Casino Express*, the ship was again advertised for sale in August 2004. *Author's collection*

Opposite: During September 1989 Sealink British Ferries announced the acquisition of the 15,001 grt *Visby* for the Fishguard–Rosslare service. The ship was the largest ferry ever to operate on the Irish Sea, and with capacity for 1600 passengers and 517 cars she finally brought the service out of the shadow of the Holyhead route. Before replacing the *St Brendan*, the ship sailed to Tilbury for a £2m refit. Dressed overall, resplendent in Sealink colours and under her new name *Felicity*, the ship arrived at Rosslare for the first time on 2 March 1990, passing the *St Brendan* on her morning sailing to Wales. The *Felicity* entered service on 5 March and immediately endeared herself to the travelling public. Her ability to swallow copious amounts of freight was a huge draw card and literally overnight Sealink's traffic figures on the route began to rocket. No sooner had the *Felicity* entered service than the bulk of Sealink British Ferries was sold to the Swedish Stena Line. To reflect the change in ownership the ship was renamed *Stena Felicity* (see page 131) and the new brand name Sealink Stena Line was applied to her hull during a £0.5m refit. In November 1990 she is seen leaving Fishguard for dry-dock as Holyhead's newly allocated *Stena Cambria* arrives to take up the run.

David Rea, courtesy Brian Cleare

Outbound in Loch Ryan for Larne is Townsend Thoresen's *Free Enterprise I*. She was transferred to the Larne–Cairnryan service as the main passenger ship in 1975 but she was not a success and was replaced in 1976 by the larger *Free Enterprise IV*. Sold by Townsend Thoresen to Greek operator Ventouris in February 1980 the ship embarked on a long and varied career in warmer climes. Amazingly, during 2004 she was still in service, operating during the summer months between Crete and Santorini as the *Kallisti*. *Nigel Thorntonn collection*

Opposite: The 1976 season brought the *Free Enterprise IV* north from the English Channel. Built in 1970 the ship entered service on the North Channel on 20 May 1976 and she became an instant success, establishing a record for the fastest crossing from Cairnryan to Larne with a berth-to-berth time of one hour 41 minutes. The ship returned again in 1977 by which time she had been fully allocated to the service, remaining on the North Channel (apart from winter relief on the North Sea) until 1986. On 10 July 1986 the ship left Larne for the last time, bound for Dover. The entry into service of the new *Pride of Calais* rendered the 'FE IV' redundant and on 4 December 1987 she was withdrawn and laid up pending sale. After one final swansong back at Dover she was sold for service between Denmark and Germany in April 1988. Today the ship is in service between Egypt and Saudi Arabia, as the *Tag El Salam*. *Author's collection*

Freshly released at Dover by new and larger tonnage the *Free Enterprise III* opened Townsend Thoresen's new seasonal Larne–Cairnryan passenger service on 1 July 1974. Famed for their fresh approach to the Channel services, particularly when compared with what many considered to be the rather stale ships of the nationalised operators at Dover, Townsend Thoresen sought to bring their English Channel successes to the 'tired' Irish services. However all was not plain sailing and that first season was dogged by delayed sailings, primarily due to insufficient turnaround times at both ports. This was the *Free Enterprise III*'s one and only stint on the North Channel although she returned to the Irish Sea in 1985 as the ill-fated *Mona's Isle* (see page 97). In this view she is seen arriving at Dover in her original livery.   *Ian Collard*

The first of four similar ships ordered from Harland & Wolff for Sealink's North Channel, Dover Straits and Irish Sea routes, the *Galloway Princess* entered service between Stranraer and Larne on 1 May 1980, ten months later than scheduled. With her impressive capacity for freight on twin decks the ship was an immediate success and indeed during her first four months in service Sealink's market share on the Scotland–Northern Ireland passage rose by some 8%. (See also *Stena Galloway*, pages 132 and 133)

Jack Phelan

Brittany Ferries' *Goelo* appeared in Irish waters on only one occasion. On 15 March 1981 she operated a Roscoff–Cork round trip in place of the *Armorique*. After a somewhat varied career she eventually became the *Sardegna Bella* operating between Livorna and Olbia for Sardegna Line. She was sold for breaking in July 2001.

Jack Phelan

The *Gotland* is pictured arriving at Rosslare at the end of a passage from Cherbourg. Brittany Ferries' chartered *Gotland* made her debut in Irish waters in late 1988 when she was sub-chartered by the Irish Continental Group to maintain their Rosslare–Le Havre/Cherbourg routes and also Belfast Ferries' Belfast–Liverpool service while the regular ships were overhauled.

Sean Martley

Opposite: In Sealink British Ferries livery the *Galloway Princess* breaks away from Larne on a murky spring day in 1989. During her Sealink years the ship led an uneventful life, never straying from the route for which she was built. However under Stena stewardship she did venture onto other Irish Sea crossings.

Author

Following the loss of the *Princess Victoria* the train ferry *Hampton Ferry* of 1934 was transferred to Stranraer from the Southern Region of British Railways. Each summer from June 1953 to 1961 the ship came north to maintain the seasonal car ferry service and provide support to the passenger steamer *Princess Margaret*. On the route for which she was built the *Hampton Ferry* accommodated twelve sleeping cars and two baggage trucks. The after end of the train deck and two side tracks were flushed in to allow cars to be carried. In addition to the main train deck, cars could also be carried on the upper deck which was accessed at Dover and Dunkerque via side loading ramps. Space was available for up to 800 passengers. With the arrival of the *Caledonian Princess* in December 1961 the 'Hampton' remained at Dover in 1962 and she was eventually withdrawn from service in 1969.

Nigel Thorntonn collection

Opposite: The *Hengist* is seen alongside at Rosslare on 7 October 1985 after her first morning arrival from Fishguard. This was the *Hengist*'s first spell of Irish Sea service and came following engine trouble in the *St Brendan*. She remained on the link until 17 November. The *Hengist* was actually earmarked as Holyhead's second ship in 1981, pending delivery of the new *St David* from Harland & Wolff. However strong protests from the Dover Strait prevented the move and the steamer *Earl Siward* was sent around instead. (See also *Stena Hengist*, page 135)

Brian Cleare

A familiar shape returned to Cork Harbour on 14 March 1992, the former Brittany Ferries vessel *Cornouailles* (see page 34). Now owned by British Channel Island Ferries and renamed *Havelet*, her brief return on charter to open the Brittany Ferries season, is certainly well remembered by all connected with the Roscoff service, but for the wrong reasons. During her sailing to the French port she was hit by a large sea causing trucks to overturn on her vehicle deck. With a heavy list the Master managed to bring his ship about and make a slow and cautious return to Cork where the contents of her vehicle deck – damaged trucks and twisted cars – were removed. The *Havelet* left Cork under something of a cloud on 16 March and was never again seen in Irish waters. British Channel Island Ferries' services were later taken over by Condor Ferries and the *Havelet* was eventually sold for service in Montenegro.

Gary Davies/Maritime Photographic

In 1964 British Rail brought the Holyhead–Dun Laoghaire route into the car ferry age with an order for a new ship from Hawthorn Leslie (Shipbuilders) Ltd. Built at a cost of £1.6m she was the first of two ships which were to be the last turbine steamers for the railway company and saddled with the unimaginative name of *Holyhead Ferry 1*, she was launched on 17 February 1965. Her half-sister, *Dover,* was ordered from Swan Hunter for the English Channel and she beat the Irish Sea ship into service by one month. The new service opened for business on 9 July 1965, not with the *Holyhead Ferry 1*, which was late from her builders, but the newly converted *Normannia* from the Dover–Boulogne run. The *Holyhead Ferry 1* finally took over on 19 July. During the height of the summer season one round trip was offered daily, departing Holyhead at 1045 and Dun Laoghaire at 1530. At weekends an additional round trip was offered, leaving the Welsh port at 2015 and from Dun Laoghaire at 0600. The service was a rampant success but even so it was still a seasonal affair and in mid-October the route reverted to mail ship operation until the summer of 1966. With the mail ship *Hibernia* resting alongside Dun Laoghaire's departure berth the *Holyhead Ferry 1* leaves on a 1530 sailing to Holyhead in summer 1968. The new car ferry could accommodate 153 averaged size cars on her vehicle deck which was equipped with a turntable forward and aft to assist with positioning cars ready for disembarkation. A small mezzanine deck was accessed by hydraulically operated ramps port and starboard. Two hatches were also fitted fore and aft, primarily for loading mail into the ship but also to allow cars to be lifted out should the stern door fail. Passenger capacity was 1000 and 64 berths were available in a variety of cabins. Having completed her first season the *Holyhead Ferry 1* took on the role of winter relief ship and on 14 February 1966 she made her first appearance on the Stranraer–Larne service, remaining there for one month before returning to her Welsh home port. Apart from the gradual extension of her Holyhead season this routine pretty much continued for the rest of the 1960s. During the winter of 1968/69 she found herself sailing on the mail service departing Holyhead on the time honoured 0315 sailing on Mondays, Wednesdays and Fridays. (See also *Earl Leofric*, page 46)

Ian Collard

Opposite: In 1973 the *Holyhead Ferry 1* had her first spell of English Channel service after which she relieved Fishguard's *Caledonian Princess* for annual overhaul and she is seen here arriving at the Welsh port from Rosslare. By now the 'Ferry 1' found her self based at Dover with that port's *Dover* being based at Holyhead! The reason was the latter's greater car capacity over her half-sister. The confusion ended in 1976 when the *Holyhead Ferry 1* was sent to Swan Hunter on the Tyne for conversion to drive through operation from which she emerged renamed *Earl Leofric*.

Jim Ashby

The *Horsa* is pictured here just off Holyhead's North Stack in June 1990. Built for Sealink's Folkestone services in 1972 the ship was transferred to the Irish Sea in March 1990, initially to replace the chartered *Lady of Mann* which was maintaining the link in place of the fire damaged *St Columba*. On 23 May she reintroduced a seasonal two-ship passenger service on the Dun Laoghaire run. She was a popular addition to the route and to give her an Irish Sea 'feel' many of her lounges were named after Welsh and Irish towns and regions. Having finished her summer season on 5 September, the *Horsa* took up the Fishguard–Rosslare service while the *Felicity* was off for mechanical attention. Her time on the route was a brief affair as a breakdown in the *St Columba* on 12 September forced new company owners Sealink Stena Line to return the *Felicity* to service and dispatch the *Horsa* back to Holyhead and the Dun Laoghaire run. The *St Columba* finally returned to service on 12 October after which the *Horsa* returned to the Folkestone–Boulogne crossing. (See also *Stena Horsa, page 136*)   *Author*

Putting in a brief appearance on the Stranraer–Belfast service in April 1993 was the *Hoverspeed Boulogne*. (See also *SeaCat Isle of Man*, page 114)

Author's collection

A whole new concept in ferry travel arrived in the Irish Sea in November 1990 when Sea Containers, who at that time held over 40% equity in the Isle of Man Steam Packet Company, announced they were to bring their new 74 metre High Speed Wave Piercing Catamaran, *Hoverspeed Great Britain*, to the Isle of Man for a promotional visit. Departing Milford Haven for the northwards passage at around 0700 hours meant an arrival into Douglas at around noon. The Steam Packet's Marine Superintendent, Capt Peter Corrin said, "The true realisation of speed came when abeam of the South Stack (off Holyhead) at 1040 hours we gave an ETA to Douglas of 1200 hours, a distance of some 50 miles being covered in little over an hour." Her arrival in Douglas was greeted by a large number of people gathered at various points from Douglas Head and around the Bay. By the time the craft departed for Portsmouth on Thursday 8 November she had generated sufficient interest for the Manx public to campaign for a regular fast craft service. With the establishment of high speed services on the Irish Sea the *Hoverspeed Great Britain* was to see service on the Stranraer–Belfast route for the summer of 1993. On 29 March 2001 she took up the seasonal Heysham–Belfast crossing, during which time she also appeared on the Isle of Man Steam Packet's Manx routes from time to time.

Gary Davies/Maritime Photographic

Left: The German-built *Innisfallen (IV)*, the fourth ship to take the traditional name of the British & Irish Steam Packet Company's Cork-based passenger ships, entered service between Cork and Swansea on 2 May 1969. As the vessel broke away from the Tivoli terminal at 2100 hrs sharp, other nearby ships sounded their whistles in salute to the newcomer. Along the banks of the River Lee cars stopped and people lined the roads at Blackrock as the ship, under the command of Capt Tom Davies, sailed past on her maiden voyage. This was the new breed of Irish Sea car ferry, sweeping away the homely comforts of the old favourites of years gone by. In an age of intensive schedules with relatively short turnaround times, utilitarian and easy to clean accommodation was now the order of the day. Described as Western Europe's fastest car ferry the 24.5 knots ship cost IR£2.5m and offered accommodation for 1200 passengers and 240 cars. Following the introduction of the new *Connacht* in 1979 the *Innisfallen* was transferred to the Dublin–Liverpool service where she was part of a three-ship service alongside her sister *Leinster* and the *Munster*. The move was not a success, the political situation in Northern Ireland also making an impact on traffic and in January 1980 she was sold to Corsica Ferries for further trade. She was last heard of in 2004, in Turkish waters, as the *Derin Deniz*.   *Author's collection*

Above: Following the sale of the *Innisfallen (IV)* to Corsica Ferries, her sister-ship *Leinster* was replaced at Dublin by the *Connacht*. The smaller ship was renamed *Innisfallen (V)*, releasing her name for a new ship, and transferred south to maintain the Cork/Rosslare–Pembroke Dock routes. With a speed 5 knots less than her predecessor of the same name the 'false Innis', as she became known as, really struggled with the Cork leg and on 2 February 1983 the longer crossing was abandoned in favour of the four hour link from Rosslare. As we have seen, the route was tried again with the chartered *Fennia* but as far as the *Innisfallen* was concerned Cork was finished and she is seen here alongside at Rosslare in March 1985. A deal to sell the ship to Italian interests had fallen through in 1984 and she was retained to continue sailing from Rosslare. A pooling arrangement established by B&I Line and Sealink in 1985 was extended and on 5 January 1986 the Pembroke service was closed and the *Innisfallen* was laid up at Dublin. However, plans to replace the *Innisfallen* and *St Brendan* with one large 'superferry' under a single brand failed to materialise and the Irish ship found herself sailing to Fishguard as the second ship alongside the *St Brendan*. The *Innisfallen* was a poor partner for the Sealink ferry, her diminutive vehicle deck being hopelessly inadequate. With continued talk of a larger tonnage for the route the 18 year old ship was sold to Strintzis Lines of Greece at the end of the 1986 season for further service as the *Ionian Sun*. (See also *Ionian Sun*, page 62 and *Leinster (V)*, page 75)   *Author*

Having disappeared off to warmer climes, the former *Innisfallen (V)* surprised Irish Sea observers when she returned to Cork on charter
to Swansea–Cork Ferries for the 1990 season. Trading as the *Celtic Pride II*, but not officially renamed, the Greek-crewed *Ionian Sun* had
undergone some changes since her B&I days, including the replacement of her aft lounge by cabins and the extension of her boat deck right
over the stern. In true Greek style an open air swimming pool had also been fitted and it has to be said she was looking far smarter than she had
done in the last decade of B&I operation. A source of amusement on her return to Cork was an old price list found onboard showing an Irish
whiskey to be just 41p! (See also *Innisfallen (V)*, page 61 and *Leinster (V)*, page 75)   *Gary Davies/Maritime Photographic*

This is the ship that started it all on the Larne–Cairnryan route, the *Ionic Ferry*. With an increased passenger certificate for 218 she opened the new service across the North Channel in July 1973. Sold by Townsend Thoresen in 1976 the ship was finally broken up at Aliaga, Turkey in September 1988.   *Author's collection*

Opposite: Almost 15 years after she had last operated in Irish waters as the *Dragon* (see page 37) Townsend Thoresen introduced the ship onto the Larne–Cairnryan route as the *Ionic Ferry*. Prior to taking up her new role on the North Channel Townsend Thoresen sent the ship to Glasgow for a major refit which involved the removal of her cabins at the stern to allow more trucks to be carried on the upper deck. Entering service on 10 July 1986 and replacing the *Free Enterprise IV* the *Ionic Ferry* soon settled down into a regular routine alongside the freight vessel *Europic Ferry*. Following the takeover of Townsend Thoresen in December 1986 the *Ionic Ferry* was a P&O vessel once again, but it was to be another ten months before the brand name P&O European Ferries was adopted. In the meantime the *Ionic Ferry* made national news headlines on 3 June 1987 when she drifted aground while waiting off Larne in thick fog. The ship was refloated on the tide ten hours later and she sailed for dry-dock at Liverpool and repairs to a damaged propeller. By and large, though, the ship led a fairly quiet life and she served the company well until June 1992 when she was replaced by the larger *Pride of Rathlin*. Sold for further service with Greek operator Marlines as the *Viscountess M*, the ship left Larne for the final time on 11 June. Sadly her career in warmer climes came to an abrupt end on 2 March 2002 when, as the *Millennium Express II*, she was gutted by fire. Declared a constructive total loss this handsome ferry ended her days at a ship breakers yard at Aliaga, Turkey in April 2003, 15 years after the first *Ionic Ferry* ended her days at the same yard.   *Author's collection*

Illustrating B&I Line's secondary status on the southern corridor the *Isle of Inishmore (I)* is dwarfed by Stena Sealink Line's *Stena Felicity* at Rosslare in June 1994. The latter is dressed overall for the first visit to the port by the high speed craft *Stena Sea Lynx*. Following the takeover of B&I Line by the Irish Continental Group on 1 January 1992, the *Leinster (VI)* was extensively refitted at a cost of IR£3m and renamed *Isle of Inishmore* in readiness for a permanent move to the Rosslare–Pembroke route in time for the 1993 summer season. Resplendent in a new all white livery with blue stripes the ship looked smarter than ever when she switched places with the southern corridor's chartered *Isle of Innisfree*. The renaming of the *Leinster* brought the end of a long tradition of naming ships of B&I, and the old City of Dublin Steam Packet Company, after the four provinces of Ireland. An accident with the *Isle of Innisfree* whilst going alongside at Holyhead during the last week of January 1994 caused major damage to the only berth the ship could use at the port. As a result, the *Isle of Inishmore*, fresh from overhaul at Birkenhead, was pressed into service on the Dublin run. (See also *Isle of Inishturk*, pages 66 & 67 and *Leinster (VI)*, page 75)   *Author*

The *Isle of Inishmore (II)* entered service on 4 March 1997, making an immediate impact on trading figures on the Holyhead route. An impressive ship, she was some 11,000 tonnes larger than the *Isle of Innisfree (II)*. Her luxury accommodation caters for 2,200 passengers while her vehicle decks, with 2,100 lane metres, can carry 856 cars or 122 trucks or a mixture of both. When she was ordered some observers were fearful that the new ship would be too large for the Irish Sea and that Irish Ferries would struggle to fill her. However it soon became abundantly obvious that even with this huge ability to swallow up vast amounts of freight the *Isle of Inishmore* was capacity constrained. With typical foresight, Irish Ferries moved to meet growing demand and another new ship was ordered. The arrival of *Ulysses* in 2001 released the *Isle of Inishmore* from Holyhead and since then she has operated most successfully on the Rosslare–Pembroke route.

Capt Vernon Kinley

Opposite: A tug assists the *Isle of Inishmore (I)* back to her berth after the ship went aground in Rosslare during a storm in September 1995. In January of that year the Irish Ferries brand was extended to include B&I Line's services. Following her overhaul the *Isle of Inishmore* returned to service in a revised Irish Ferries livery which in addition to the familiar green funnel with flag motif now included the brand name ahead of a colourful wave design on the hull. On 14 February 1996 the ship once again found herself on the Dublin run while modifications were carried out to the Outer Harbour berth at Holyhead in preparation for the arrival of the new purpose-built *Isle of Innisfree (II)*. Having been released by the new giant on 23 May the *Isle of Inishmore* returned south. Two months later came the announcement that Dublin's new ship would move to Rosslare in 1997 when an even larger vessel would enter service to Holyhead, Irish Ferries were making their presence felt and the *Isle of Inishmore*'s days were numbered. The new ship was to be named *Isle of Inishmore (II)* and to release the name the former *Leinster (VI)* was renamed *Isle of Inishturk* (see pages 66 and 67) on 5 November 1996.

Brian Cleare

16 February 1997 saw the *Isle of Inishturk* off Rosslare taking the full force of an Irish Sea gale in her stride. These three shots taken from the *Stena Felicity* by well known marine artist Brian Cleare really do speak for themselves and serve as a fitting tribute to a fine ship that provided 16 years of reliable between Ireland, England and Wales. On March 22 1997 the ship stood down from service and sailed for lay up at Le Havre pending sale. She did not have long to wait and in June she was sold to the Canadian Government and renamed *Madeline* for the CTMA service between Prince Edward Island and the Magdalen Islands. (See also *Isle of Inishmore (I)*, page 64 and *Leinster (VI)*, page 75) *Brian Cleare*

One of the first moves by the Irish Continental Group following their purchase of B&I Line was to address the company's outdated fleet. The Rosslare–Pembroke service had for many years been in dire need of suitable tonnage and in 1991 the route was finally allocated a ship with which to seriously compete against the *Stena Felicity* on the rival Stena Sealink route to Fishguard. The chartered ship was the *Stena Nautica*, formerly Danish State Rail's *Niels Klim*, but more interestingly owned by Sealink's new parent Stena Line! Replacing the *Munster*, the newcomer, renamed *Isle of Innisfree (I),* boasted accommodation for 2000 passengers and over 400 cars. The ship had transferred to the Holyhead run early in 1993 but she moved south again in January 1994. Although not entirely suitable for the Irish Sea routes, her slow speed of just 17 knots being a major factor, she was an important step in the regeneration of the former state-owned company.   *Author*

Awaiting a departing cruise ship the *Isle of Innisfree (II)* holds position in Dublin Bay before proceeding up the River Liffey. Offering accommodation for 1650 passengers the ship brought state-of-the-art facilities in a variety of lounges spread over three decks. On the vehicle decks space was provided for some 600 cars, or 108 trucks or 100 trucks and 50 cars. She was an instant success with the travelling public and with rapidly rising traffic levels Irish Ferries soon announced another new build which would release the 1996-built *Isle of Innisfree* to replace the *Isle of Inishturk* at Rosslare from March 1997. On the Pembroke run the *Isle of Innisfree* was again somewhat a victim of her own success and full sailings were a frequent occurrence. Replaced by the *Isle of Inishmore (II)* in May 2001, the *Isle of Innisfree* was laid up at Dublin before moving to Le Havre for lay-up pending charter. A planned deal with an Italian operator fell through, but not before retouched photos of the ship in a new livery appeared in their publicity material. In March 2003 she was chartered by P&O for the Portsmouth–Cherbourg service as Pride of Cherbourg.   *Author*

The monohull fast craft *Jetliner*, P&O's first venture into high speed car ferry operations, arrives at Larne from Cairnryan. The craft was introduced onto the North Channel in June 1996 and gained a reputation for being somewhat unreliable. Quite often the craft ran on just three of her four engines, the result of numerous technical problems. On one occasion, 5 April 1997, she had to be towed back into Larne when two gearboxes failed on passage. Despite her problems and poor sea-keeping, *Jetliner* can be accredited with building traffic on the route thanks to her fast 60 minutes crossing time. Not surprisingly her four year charter was not renewed and in June 2000 she was replaced by the high speed catamaran *SuperStar Express*. After almost a year in lay-up at Bergen the vessel was chartered to Indonesia's PT Pelni for service between Semarang, Pontianak and Taijung.
Author

Opposite top: Irish Ferries entered the fast craft era with the 'DUBLINSwift' service in 1999. Built at a cost of IR£29 million, the *Jonathan Swift*'s speed of 39 knots reduced the crossing time from Dublin City to Holyhead to just 1 hour 49 minutes. The craft offers space for 800 passengers and 200 cars. The *Jonathan Swift* arrived into Dublin Port after a 23-day voyage from the Austal yard in Fremantle, Australia on 5 May 1999. Under the command of Captains Tony Canavan, Steve Hutson and Paul Devaney and with a complement of twenty crew, her route home was via the Indian Ocean, Suez Canal, Mediterranean and through the Bay of Biscay with stops along the way for refuelling. Passing the brand new *Ulysses*, inbound from Finland on her delivery voyage, in Dublin's River Liffey, the 86 metre *Jonathan Swift* is dwarfed by the 208 metre giant.

Author

Opposite bottom: The Isle of Man Steam Packet's *King Orry* is pictured swinging in Douglas harbour after arriving on an afternoon sailing from Heysham in June 1994. The entry into service of the *King Orry* in December 1990 was a proud occasion for the Isle of Man Steam Packet Company, then in its 160th year of operation. For the next eight years the ship performed admirably, coping with the foulest of winter weather as she maintained the lifeline service to the Isle of Man. Until the availability of the multi-user ferry terminal at Dublin's Berth 49 the *King Orry* also made appearances at Dun Laoghaire with Douglas sailings over the Christmas and Easter holidays. During her final days with the Steam Packet the *King Orry* spent some time on the Liverpool–Dublin service when the fast craft *SuperSeaCat Two* was withdrawn for technical attention. On 21 September 1998 she made her final departure from Dublin in ballast after an overnight sailing from Liverpool. One week later, on 28 September, the *King Orry* completed her final commercial Heysham–Douglas sailing. The following day she sailed for lay-up at Birkenhead pending sale and on 23 October she left the Irish Sea for the last time. Sold for £2m she now operates for the Italian Moby Line as the *Moby Love*.

Author

Seen from the *Stena Felicity* in Milford Haven the *Koningin Beatrix* sails for Rosslare from Pembroke on 27 June 1997, her first day in service in Irish waters. In severe gales the 'Felicity' had diverted from Fishguard with 1171 passengers when it became obvious she could not berth at the port, while the newcomer could not use her new home port until ramp modifications had been completed. It was not until 3 July that the changeover took place, the *Koningin Beatrix*'s maiden sailing from Fishguard departing for Rosslare five hours late. At the time she was the largest ferry to ever operate on St George's Channel. Although a very well appointed ship the *Koningin Beatrix* did not enjoy the same level of success as her predecessor. She soon earned a reputation for being rather difficult to handle and indeed on 3 August 1997 she demolished a section of the harbour wall at Rosslare while attempting to berth in an ENE Force 9. Having waited off the port all night for an improvement in the weather the ship proceeded to Dublin where she disembarked her 1200 passengers 20 hours after they left Fishguard. Before she was replaced by the *Stena Europe* on 13 March 2002 the 'KB' saw more trips to Dublin in adverse weather conditions and at one stage even put in an appearance on the Holyhead run. Another unusual diversion was on 13 July 1998 when she put in a passage from Cork to Roscoff, on charter, to transfer people and equipment connected with the Irish leg of the Tour de France race.

Brian Cleare

The splendid *Lady of Mann* powers away from Douglas early in her career. The fourth car ferry for the Isle of Man Steam Packet Company and a sister of the earlier *Mona's Queen*, the *Lady of Mann* entered service between Douglas and Liverpool on 30 June 1976. The ship was very different from other new ferries of that era. For their new ship the Steam Packet elected to continue with the side loading system first introduced with the *Manx Maid* in 1962, although that was not just due to the fact that Douglas did not have a linkspan, but also because it provided great flexibility to handle the ship at just about any quay wall at any port, as the author found out in 1999 when he handled the ship on a cargo berth in Dublin when she lost her slot at Ferryport. Despite being labelled as 'outdated' when built she has outlasted many UK ferries built around the same time. While the Liverpool service was the 'bread and butter' crossing until 1985, when the Mersey was abandoned in favour of Heysham, the *Lady of Mann* also maintained seasonal sailings to Dublin, Belfast and Fleetwood.

Author's collection

As built, the *Lady of Mann*'s accommodation could be best described as 'traditional', but early in 1989 the ship was rebuilt. Her entire accommodation was gutted and then refitted in a style never before seen on a Steam Packet ship. Gone were painted steel bulkheads and wooden bench seating. When she returned to operation on a reinstated Liverpool route on 26 May 1989 the *Lady of Mann* was ready for at least another ten years service. Seen here displaying her then new Steam Packet livery, the *Lady of Mann*, under the command of Marine Manager Capt Peter Corrin, arrives at Warrenpoint for an excursion sailing to Douglas on 16 June 2000. Since 1998 the ship's years have basically consisted of winter service from Douglas, a round the island cruise and occasional summer excursions to ports such as Whitehaven, Llandudno and Warrenpoint, a hectic schedule during the Manx TT, followed by a charter in the Azores before returning to the Irish Sea ready for another winter. There can be no question, the *Lady of Mann* is one of the most successful of all car ferries on the Irish Sea. From day one she has operated with a reputation for dependability and reliability. To further extend her years the ship underwent another major refit early in 2001 enabling her to comply with the latest Safety Of Life At Sea (SOLAS) regulations. For how many more years the ship will grace the Irish Sea is not certain, but until the day of her withdrawal dawns she will undoubtedly continue to serve with the reliability that has endeared her to so many passengers and friends and the Isle of Man Steam Packet Company.

Author

The *Lagan Viking* was introduced onto the Liverpool–Belfast service by Norse Irish Ferries on 16 November 1997. Owned by Lavantia Transport of Italy, part of the Visentini Group, both she and her sister *Mersey Viking* were initially chartered but bought outright in 2001. Primarily a freight vessel, she is capable of accommodating some 340 passengers and on that basis she is included in this book. Her impressive vehicle decks have space for 130 trailers and 100 cars.

Ian Collard

Sporting the livery of the merged Norse Irish Ferries and Merchant Ferries, the *Lagan Viking* is outbound from Liverpool on her eight hour passage to Belfast. The ship will be transferred to the Liverpool–Dublin route in 2005.

Ian Collard

Entering service between Dublin and Liverpool on 1 June 1969 the new IR£2.5m *Leinster (V)* combined comfortable cabins with spacious lounges and a car deck with bow and stern doors. She led a fairly quiet life on the route, only straying to the southern Cork–Swansea service to provide overhaul relief for her sister *Innisfallen*. With the sale of her sister in January 1980 the *Leinster* took the name *Innisfallen (V)* and transferred to the St George's Channel in September 1980. (See also *Innisfallen (V)*, page 61 and *Ionian Sun*, page 62)   *Ian Collard*

B+I Line's *Leinster (VI)* entered service in June 1981 after a very public war of words between the operator and builder, Verolme Cork Dockyard, over a late delivery. B+I threatened to refuse acceptance of the ship but in the event she made her debut between Dublin and Liverpool at the height of the season.   *Author's collection*

Early Ro/Ro days at Rosslare and a truck is seen driving off the French registered *Leopard* after a crossing from Le Havre in June 1968, the first month of ferry services between Ireland and France. Despite the high carryings the service was not continued beyond 1971 as both the *Leopard* and sister *Dragon* were required on the English Channel.

Author's collection

Burns & Laird's *Lion* goes astern on Belfast's River Lagan before turning for Ardrossan. On 12 February 1976 she made her last crossing before closing the Belfast–Ardrossan passenger service and transferring to the English Channel for further operation with Normandy Ferries. A rather plain looking ship, she had capacity for 160 cars and 1200 passengers.

Ian Collard

England's first purpose-built stern loading car ferry first appeared in service on the Irish Sea in 1971. The *Lord Warden* of 1952 spent that summer in service between Holyhead and Dun Laoghaire but it is probably her spell on the short-lived Fishguard–Dun Laoghaire route between July and September 1978 for which she is best remembered. In this view, with the newly chartered *Stena Normandica* arriving from Rosslare, the *Lord Warden* is seen leaving for the Co Wexford port. Under the command of Capt John Bakewell the *Lord Warden*'s last passenger sailing under the Sealink flag was from Dun Laoghaire to Holyhead on 8 September 1979. After lay-up at Newhaven she was sold for further service in the Red Sea but by 1981 she was under the cutter's torch at a breakers yard in Pakistan. *Brian Cleare*

This rare photo of Weymouth's *Maid of Kent* alongside at Dun Laoghaire on 3 November 1979 was taken by Cork's 'Man of Ships' Jack Phelan. This was her one and only time on the Holyhead run but she had previously operated on the Irish Sea in April 1975 when she covered for the *Ailsa Princess* on the Stranraer–Larne service, and also in March and October 1976 when she relieved the *Dover* at Fishguard. *Jack Phelan*

It could only be an Isle of Man steamer! The graceful *Manx Maid*, her steam whistle in full flight, arrives at Douglas from Fleetwood on 27 August 1981. Built in 1962 she was the Isle of Man Steam Packet's first car ferry, entering service on 23 May that year. It was not unusual to see the *Manx Maid* and her fleetmates on the west side of the Island during periods of easterly gales when berthing at Douglas became untenable. Peel was the Steam Packet's standby port and the company's staff were quite adept at handling the diversions, normally at very short notice. Invariably the ship would arrive alongside a pier lined with buses ready to transport the somewhat ashen-faced passengers to the sanctuary of their homes after a gruelling sea voyage. At the end of the 1984 season the *Manx Maid* was withdrawn from service, her final sailing from Douglas to Liverpool being taken by Capt Vernon Kinley. She was sold for static use in Bristol early the following year. Sadly plans for the ship fell through and during the spring of 1986 she was broken up at Garston.

Richard Danielson

What can one say about the *Manx Viking* other than her arrival at Douglas for berthing trials (as the *Monte Castillo)* on 22 December 1977 set in motion the greatest shock wave to hit the venerable Isle of Man Steam Packet Company since its inception in 1830. After several delays the *Manx Viking* opened the new Manx Line operation on 26 August 1978, providing for the first time a full Ro/Ro service to the Isle of Man. If ever a ship had a baptism of fire it was this one and after numerous technical problems the company was rescued by James Fisher & Sons and Sealink UK Ltd.

Author's collection

Following the 1985 merger between the Isle of Man Steam Packet and Sealink the *Manx Viking* returned to Douglas, after annual overhaul, in Isle of Man Steam Packet colours, on 21 January 1986. This was to be her final year on the Irish Sea and at the end of September she quietly slipped away from Douglas for the last time.

Stan Basnett

Opposite top: The *Mona's Queen* leaves Dun Laoghaire for Holyhead while on charter to Sealink British Ferries following a fire in the *St David* in April 1988. The Isle of Man Steam Packet's first diesel passenger ship entered service between Douglas and Liverpool on 8 June 1972. Based on the earlier steam powered side loading car ferries the *Mona's Queen* opened the new seasonal car ferry service to Douglas on 4 July of that year. In 1974 she inaugurated car ferry sailings to Dublin and two years later she did the same for Fleetwood. Her spell on charter to Sealink at Holyhead was not the ship's only sortie away from home. In September 1989 she found herself at Cherbourg catering for 1000 passengers at the start of the Round the World Yacht Race. This complete she was pressed into service for Sealink once again, this time on their Western Channel routes in place of first the *Earl Granville* and then *Earl Godwin*. At the end of her 1990 season the 'Queen' was laid up at Birkenhead pending sale. Some five years passed before a buyer was found and on 4 December 1995 she left the Mersey for the last time, bound for the Philippines and a new career as *Mary The Queen*. *Author*

Opposite bottom: The Isle of Man Steam Packet's *Ben-my-Chree (V)* is shown here alongside at Douglas. Built in 1966 it was to be another 12 years before her Masters were to have the luxury of a bow thrust unit. Until then both the 'Ben' and her sister *Manx Maid* often required assistance from a tug to lift off a berth in windy conditions. *Ian Collard*

Above: Norse Irish Ferries' *Mersey Viking* alongside at Belfast's Victoria Terminal 2. Along with her twin sister, the *Lagan Viking*, these two ships brought a new era of travel to the Liverpool–Belfast service after years of under investment by previous operators. *Author*

(continued on page 97)

The *Caledonian Princess* leaves Larne for Stranraer in 1967 wearing the full livery of British Rail.

Ian Collard

Seen from the bridge, the *Holyhead Ferry 1* takes on the might of the Irish Sea in April 1969.

Capt Walter Lloyd-Williams

The *Lord Warden* leaves Dun Laoghaire for Fishguard on 15 July 1978.   *Jack Phelan*

The *Avalon* steams into Dublin Bay with an evening arrival from Holyhead in May 1976.   *Robert Matheson/Author's collection*

In September 1976 *Dover* sweeps out of Dun Laoghaire Harbour for Holyhead while, in the background, *Duke of Lancaster* begins her run astern to her berth. To meet the demand for freight space *Dover* was converted to drive-through operation in 1977, and renamed *Earl Siward* she returned to Dover Strait operations.

Robert Matheson/Author's collection

With clouds of black smoke the *Maid of Kent* goes astern through Dun Laoghaire harbour in 1979.

Jack Phelan

Alongside at Stranraer's Mail Pier the *Antrim Princess* clearly displays the extension added to the after end of her accommodation to increase the second class passenger spaces during her 1974 refit at Holyhead.

Stan Basnett

31 January 1982 and *Ailsa Princess* and *Manx Viking* are seen together at Douglas. *Manx Viking* was departing for Falmouth, leaving *Ailsa Princess* to take up the Heysham service.

Richard Danielson

Summer 1984 and the *St David* lies alongside Holyhead's Town Quay. In the background are the container ships *Rhodri Mawr* and *Brian Boroime*.

Author

B&I Line's chartered *Stena Germanica* rests alongside Cork's Tivoli terminal in 1978. On 15 February 1985 she grounded on a reef off Puerto Rico. Declared a total loss she was broken up on site four years later.

Jack Phelan

Opposite top: With the *Lady of Mann* alongside the Victoria Pier the *King Orry* arrives at Douglas on an afternoon sailing from Heysham in June 1994. *King Orry* entered service in December 1990; that year also saw the Isle of Man Steam Packet Company celebrate its 160th year of operation. She performed well and coped with almost everything the Irish Sea could throw at her. On 28 September 1998, the *King Orry* completed her final commercial Heysham–Douglas sailing and the following day she sailed to Birkenhead for lay-up pending sale. (See also *Channel Entente*, page 31 and *Saint Eloi*, page 109) *Author*

Opposite bottom: The *Stena Hibernia* moves onto the berth in Dun Laoghaire following the departure of the *Stena Cambria*. From 1 January 1996 the Sealink name was dropped in favour of Stena Line and to erase any historic links with the old company the *Stena Hibernia* became *Stena Adventurer (I)* when she received her new livery later that month. *Author*

Under the command of Capt Kevin Flynn Irish Ferries *Saint Patrick II* approaches Cork's Ringaskiddy terminal at the end of a passage from Roscoff, during which she had diverted to assist a vessel in distress. *Author*

Lights ablaze, the *Saint Killian II* and *Felicity* rest alongside at Rosslare in March 1990.

Sean Martley, courtesy Brian Cleare

In March 1991 Capt John Sinnott brings the newly renamed *Stena Hibernia* up to Holyhead's Station Berth for the first time. On the right the *Stena Cambria*, under Capt Ray Veno, lies at the container terminal having vacated the linkspan after arrival from Dun Laoghaire.

Author

This picture shows the *Stena Antrim* swinging at Larne. On 11 November 1995 the last crossings were made between the Co Antrim port of Larne and Stranraer. The final sailing from Larne to Stranraer was operated by the *Stena Antrim* and brought to an end 123 years of service between the two ports, the new Belfast–Stranraer operation commencing the following day. In the spring of 1998 the *Stena Antrim* was withdrawn and after two months laid up was sold for service between Algeciras and Tangier as the *Ibn Batouta*. (See also *St Christopher,* page 119)

Author

Hoverspeed Great Britain visited the Isle of Man in 1990 and the Isle of Man Steam Packet Company subsequently chartered sister craft *SeaCat Boulogne*. Renamed *SeaCat Isle of Man*, 'Boulogne' entered service on 28 June 1994 and her first season was extremely successful. *She then spent the winter operating on sub-charter between Stranraer and Belfast before moving south to the English Channel and spending time with Condor Ferries. It was then back to Manx routes in May 1995 for another season. Despite being a success SeaCat Isle of Man was returned to Sea Containers at the end of the 1995 season, leaving the Isle of Man was without a fast craft in 1996.*
                                                                                                    Barry Watts

Seen from the end of Fishguard breakwater the *Koningin Beatrix* arrives from Rosslare in 1997.   *Author*

At the start of the day Stena Line's *Stena Challenger* arrives in Dublin Bay from Holyhead in summer 2000. Prior to her transfer to the Irish Sea in September 1996 the ship made a name for herself on the Dover to Dunkerque and Calais routes. *Author*

2 June 2004 and the *European Causeway* is caught by the photographer, in Loch Ryan, heading for Larne. *Norman Johnston*

Straight to the heart of Liverpool, as *SuperSeaCat Two* arrives from Dublin in 2003. The ability of the Isle of Man Steam Packet's vessels to operate to and from the Pier Head landing stage provides passengers from Douglas and Dublin with a true link straight to the city centre. They don't come any more direct than this!

Ian Collard

High speed at Holyhead as Stena Line's *Stena Explorer* passes the inbound Irish Ferries' *Jonathan Swift*.

Gary Davies/Maritime Photographic

Stena Line's *Stena Lynx III* arrives at Rosslare in June 2003. In the absence of a traditional funnel the Stena Line logo is carried on the marine evacuation system door.

Gary Davies/Maritime Photographic

In the shadow of the well-known Royal Liver building and under a threatening sky, Ian Collard captures the *Lady of Mann* stemming the tide off Liverpool's Landing Stage. In this view the ship is wearing the unpopular livery introduced by the Steam Packet's then owners Sea Containers. upon the sale of the historic company in 2003 the 'Lady' regained her traditional funnel colours, with a deeper black top giving an altogether more balanced appearance.

Ian Collard

Irish Ferries' *Ulysses* is named in honour of James Joyce's 'Ulysses', the book that immortalised the life of Dublin on 16 June 1904. Built in the shipyard of Aker Finnyards in Rauma, Finland, at a total cost of €100 million, *Ulysses* stands 12 decks high and towers over other vessels at a height of 51 metres from keel to mast. With almost three miles of parking space for 1,342 cars or 240 articulated trucks per sailing no other passenger car ferry in the world can match her vehicle carrying capacity.

Author

The impressive *Stena Adventurer (II)* arrives in Dublin during her first month in service.

Gary Davies/Maritime Photographic

Captured by a young Justin Merrigan, in persistent rain and poor light, the Isle of Man Steam Packet's *Mona's Isle* is pictured at Dun Laoghaire awaiting departure on her maiden commercial voyage to Douglas on 4 April 1985. Although a poor shot it is worthy of inclusion as a strike had prevented the *Lady of Mann* from carrying out the scheduled Easter sailing to and from Dublin and so the new flagship was sent to Ireland instead, but to Dun Laoghaire and not Dublin as the latter did not have a linkspan available for Steam Packet use. For almost one hour she put on a most unusual display as she tried to get alongside. At one point both anchors were dropped to prevent a collision with the port's East Pier as technical problems caused havoc with her approach. She eventually made it, much to the relief of all those watching from ashore, and she returned on two more occasions the following week. The company's new, and indeed first, passenger Ro/Ro ship was no stranger to the Irish Sea having operated between Cairnryan and Larne as the Townsend Thoresen's *Free Enterprise III* (see page 53). However her new role under the Manx flag was a short-lived and unhappy affair; serious deadweight problems following a major refit rendered her useless. She was atrocious to handle, as evidenced by her display at Dun Laoghaire, and she was regularly in all sorts of trouble while trying to get alongside at both ends of her Douglas–Heysham route. The decision to withdraw the ship was taken and after just one season she was stood down on 5 October 1985 and sent to Birkenhead, in disgrace, to lay-up pending sale.   *Author*

Three years after the introduction of the steamer *Holyhead Ferry 1* on British Rail's Holyhead–Dun Laoghaire route B+I Line took delivery of the first Ro/Ro passenger car ferry to fly the Irish flag, the sleek German-built *Munster (V)*. Originally laid down for Lion Ferry the hull was taken over by B+I Line for Irish Sea service. Entering service on the new B+I Motorway crossing between Dublin and Liverpool on 15 May 1968 the motor ship, resplendent in the company's bright new blue and white livery, was by far more advanced than any other ferry then operating on the Irish Sea.

Author's collection

During the Sealink British Ferries years at Holyhead there were often rumours of the Harwich–Hook of Holland ferry *St Nicholas* moving to the Irish Sea as a replacement for the *St Columba*. Not surprisingly such a move never occurred but the *St Nicholas* did eventually make it, not just to the Irish Sea, but also to the Irish flag. Acquired by Irish Ferries in January 1998, initially on a 21 month charter, the *Normandy* underwent a major refit at Dublin before taking over the Rosslare–Pembroke service from the *Isle of Innisfree*, which sailed for overhaul. With the short sea ships overhauled the *Normandy* proceeded to take up her new Rosslare–Roscoff/Cherbourg route, replacing the *Saint Killian II* and *Saint Patrick II* after many years of faithful service. This pattern of overhaul relief continues each winter with the *Normandy* being relieved at Pembroke to return to her continental sailings by early March. In 1999 the *Normandy* was purchased by Irish Ferries and she is seen here shortly afterwards alongside at Cherbourg loading for her sailing to Ireland.   *Author*

Opposite: The last B&I car ferry to carry the traditional name *Munster (VI)* entered service on the Rosslare–Pembroke service 27 March 1990. Her career under the Irish flag was a short one and having been replaced by the chartered *Isle of Innisfree (I)* she sailed to Dublin on 31 March 1992 for lay-up pending sale. After one year of idleness the ship left Dublin for the last time, under tow for Norway.

Sean Martley, courtesy Brian Cleare

This picture records the historic moment in July 1965 when a car ferry entered Dun Laoghaire for the first time to carry out a berthing trial. The ship is the *Normannia*, built in 1952 as a passenger ferry for the Southampton–Le Havre service and converted to a stern loading car ferry for the Dover–Boulogne run in 1964. On 9 July she opened the new car ferry service from Holyhead to Dun Laoghaire pending the (late) arrival of the new *Holyhead Ferry 1* from her builders. The *Normannia* stood down on 19 July and returned to the English Channel where she continued to operate until 1978 when she finished her career with relief sailings on the Weymouth–Channel Islands service. A sale for further service on the Red Sea fell through at the eleventh hour leaving the *Normannia* to remain slowly rusting away at her Newhaven lay-up berth. Finally a sale was completed and on 29 November 1978 she left the Sussex port under the command of Capt Jarvis bound for Spain and the breakers yard.

Author's collection

Smyril Line's *Norröna* was captured alongside at Dun Laoghaire in February 1994. The ship first ventured into the Irish Sea on charter to B&I Line for the Rosslare–Pembroke service in October 1989. Replacing the chartered *Earl Harold* she remained on the run until the entry into service of the *Munster (VI)* in April 1990. Before being relieved by the 'new' ship the *Norröna* hit the news headlines when a fire engulfed ten unused cabins beneath the vehicle deck, killing one member of her crew. Before finishing her B&I charter the ship operated the Dublin–Holyhead service while the *Leinster* went off for annual overhaul. The *Norröna* returned to the Irish Sea in January 1994 for a three month charter to Stena Sealink Line to cover overhaul periods on both the Fishguard and Holyhead routes. Another three month charter from January 1995 saw her based at Stranraer.   *Author*

Making her Irish debut in November 1991, one of the most unusual looking ships to offer a car ferry service across the Irish Sea has to be Norse Irish Ferries' *Norse Lagan*. With space for 140 freight units and 50 cars plus accommodation for 200 passengers the *Norse Lagan* can be credited as the ship that enabled the Belfast–Liverpool route to survive after two previous closures. She remained on the link until late 1997 and is today in service with Italian operator Moby Lines.   *Author*

Alongside at Cork's Tivoli terminal on 27 March 1981 is Brittany Ferries' *Penn-ar-Bed*. The ship first arrived in Irish waters on a flag waving exercise to the centre of Cork City on 4 May 1978. With accommodation for just 250 passengers she was used by the company to operate the quieter end of season sailings, releasing the larger *Armorique* for English Channel requirements. In 1981 Brittany Ferries sent the *Penn-ar-Bed* to Cork again, this time to open the season. She was sold for further trade in March 1984.   *Jack Phelan*

Caledonian MacBrayne's *Pioneer* was an unusual guest within the ranks of Irish Sea car ferries in June 1993. Chartered by the Isle of Man Steam Packet following a mishap with the *Lady of Mann* while she was berthing at Douglas, *Pioneer* did sterling work as she helped to keep traffic moving during the busiest two weeks in the Manx summer season, the Isle of Man TT Races.

J Aikman-Smith, courtesy Caledonian MacBrayne

Brittany Ferries' new flagship *Pont-Aven*. Entering service on the Roscoff–Cork route in spring 2004 the ship crosses in just 11 hours while passengers enjoy luxurious facilities normally only found on cruise ships. A choice of four classes of cabin – Standard, Club Class, De Luxe and Commodore is offered. All cabins, except Standard, have a flat screen TV and comfortable seating, and Commodore cabins feature patio doors and private balcony/terrace. Other on-board facilities include a pool and bar area with glass panels and panoramic windows, a wide choice of restaurants and bars, two cinemas, stylish shopping malls, live music and dancing and, of course, a special leisure area for young people. An unfortunate incident which led to the flooding of her engine room forced the withdrawal of the ship from service at the height of her first season. However, *Pont-Aven*'s excellent facilities soon saw new customer confidence in the vessel following those traumatic weeks for her owners.

Brittany Ferries

Built in 1972 for Dover services as the *Free Enterprise VI,* and renamed *Pride of Sandwich* following the takeover by Townsend Thoresen by P&O, the *Pride of Ailsa* took up service between Cairnryan and Larne on 13 March 1992. As built she was very similar to the earlier *Free Enterprise IV*, a favourite on the North Channel for ten years, but a major rebuild and stretching in 1985 put an end to that. Her final sailing on the link was on 15 June 1996 and one week later she was bound for Port Said for further trade in the Red Sea. *Author's collection*

Starting life as the *Free Enterprise VII*, the *Pride of Rathlin*'s career more or less mirrored that of the *Pride of Ailsa*. She too was 'jumboised' in 1986 and following the P&O takeover she became the *Pride of Walmer*. Renamed again for her new North Channel role the *Pride of Rathlin* entered service from Larne on 11 June 1992, allowing the withdrawal of the *Ionic Ferry*. Both the 'Rathlin' and 'Ailsa' gained excellent reputations for quality service and reliability, which went some way to compensate for their awful looks. The 'Rathlin' lasted on the link for almost four years after the departure of her sister, standing down on 11 September 2000. In this view the ship 'flashes up' for a Larne departure a couple of months before her withdrawal. *Author*

The *Prince of Brittany*'s one and only call at Cork on a scheduled car ferry service was on 3 March 1979. On this occasion she opened the 1979 Brittany Ferries season, but she did visit one other time when she called on a cruise in October 1982. The *Prince of Brittany* returned to Ireland early in 1981 but this time on charter to Irish Continental Line for the Rosslare–Cherbourg/Le Havre service while the *Saint Patrick* underwent engine repairs. Here she is eight years later arriving at Portsmouth before being renamed *Reine Mathilde*.

Gary Davies/Maritime Photographic

The *Prinsessan Desirée* arrived at Dun Laoghaire from Holyhead for the first time on 9 July 1981. The ship had just completed a stint with B+I Line on the Rosslare–Pembroke service when the Irish company sub-chartered her to Sealink pending delivery of the *St David* from builders Harland & Wolff. B+I had taken the ship on charter in May when the late arrival of the new *Leinster (VI)* delayed the *Munster*'s transfer from Dublin to Rosslare. To say they were glad to see the back of her would be an understatement for she received considerable bad press thanks to poor levels of cleanliness and time keeping, a problem which followed her to Sealink. *Robert Matheson/Author's collection*

Opposite top: Seen from the *St Brendan*, the chartered Belgian RTM Sealink ferry *Prins Philippe* is at Rosslare on 22 May 1986. With the *Innisfallen* covering the Liverpool and Holyhead routes, B&I Line chartered the 'Philippe' for three weeks as the Irish contribution to the joint Fishguard service. Despite the fact that the ship was operating on the joint Sealink/B&I service the Irish company insisted on the removal of the word 'Sealink' from her hull.

Brian Cleare

Opposite bottom: Since 1982, and before the arrival of the *Bretagne*, the *Quiberon* was the mainstay of Brittany Ferries' Roscoff–Cork seasonal service. Replacing the *Armorique* the ship represented a major capacity boost to the popular crossing, now using Ringaskiddy as the Cork terminal. The *Quiberon* was herself replaced on the Irish route by the impressive *Bretagne* in 1989.

Author

The attractive DFDS Seaways North Sea ferry *Prins Hamlet* is seen at Rosslare in March 1988 while on a ten weeks charter to B&I Line.

Brian Cleare

Sea Containers' Incat-built *Rapide* transferred to the Irish Sea from the English Channel in March 2001. Ships of the fleet never remain in one place for too long and after a season on the Liverpool–Dublin/Douglas service the 81 metre craft was transferred to the Belfast–Heysham run for 2002. With the end of the season in sight an engine room fire forced a premature withdrawal and after repairs it was yet another transfer, this time to the Belfast–Troon service where she remains in 2004. Her sister is Stena Line's *Stena Lynx III* on the Fishguard–Rosslare service. The vessel is seen here arriving in Dublin from Liverpool during the summer of 2001 and completely devoid of operator branding. Having lost her Hoverspeed livery during pre-season dry-docking, inclement weather prevented the application of her SeaCat/Steam Packet livery until well into the peak season.

Rob de Visser

This view shows Belfast Car Ferries *Saint Colum 1* inward bound in the River Mersey. Having been released from Irish Continental Line service at Rosslare the former *Saint Patrick* (see page 111) was transferred to the newly formed Irish Shipping subsidiary and as the *Saint Colum 1* she reopened a passenger car ferry service between Belfast and Liverpool on 1 May 1982. Five years later a planned sale of the ship failed to materialise, but not before she had been withdrawn and her place at Belfast taken by the *Saint Patrick II*. With her funnel repainted in Irish Ferries colours the *Saint Colum 1* returned to Rosslare and even briefly went on charter to B&I Line to provide support to the *St Brendan* on the joint service to Fishguard over the 1987 Christmas holiday. Following an internal refurbishment the *Saint Colum 1* returned to Belfast in April 1989 and remained there until the service closed in 1990. *Author's collection*

The French registered train ferry *Saint Eloi* arrives in Dun Laoghaire on 12 April 1989. Having previously completed relief duties on the Stranraer–Larne service the ship arrived at Holyhead to relieve the *St Columba* on 4 April. Her accommodation was a mess, forcing the cancellation of her first round trip to Dun Laoghaire. Having been cleaned up, complaints about her dull and spartan appearance began flooding in and on one voyage 16 protesting passengers staged a 'sit-in' in the Master's cabin. When the *St Columba* returned on 27 April there was a collective sigh of relief. The *Saint Eloi* was then dispatched to dry-dock at Falmouth for a much needed refit, from which she emerged renamed *Channel Entente*. (See also *Channel Entente*, page 31 and *King Orry*, page 70) *Author*

Built in 1973 as the *Stena Scandinavia* for Stena Line's Gothenburg to Kiel service this was the ship identified by the late Capt Coleman Raftery as being the perfect vessel to expand the Irish Continental Line fleet with an additional Rosslare–Cherbourg route. The five year old ship was duly purchased for IR£9m and in April 1978, having been briefly chartered back to Stena, she made her debut at Rosslare as the *Saint Killian*. Before entering service alongside the *Saint Patrick* the new ship visited Dun Laoghaire on a show-the-flag exercise. *Brian Cleare collection*

Alongside at Roscoff on 31 May 1997, the *Saint Killian II* displays her final Irish Ferries' livery. The Breton port was added to the network of routes in 1995. This was the ship's last year with Irish Ferries and on 27 September she sailed out of Cork for Le Havre for the final time. The following year she was sold to Cap Enterprises (Marintas) of Piræus and renamed *Medina Star*, but her intended employment failed to materialise. A lengthy period of lay-up followed until in 2002 when Hellenic Mediterranean Lines acquired her for service as out of Patras as the *Egnatia II*.   *Author*

The original livery on *Saint Patrick* consisted of a white hull with red boot topping and buff funnel. On the funnel was a St Patrick's cross on which the Fleur de Lys was superimposed. The ship opened the new Rosslare to Le Havre service on 2 June 1973. Before her 1982 transfer to Belfast Car Ferries for the new Belfast–Liverpool route, the *Saint Patrick* was chartered to B+I Line for five weeks service on the Pembroke crossing from 2 December 1981. (See also *Saint Colum I*, page 109)   *Author's collection*

Opposite: In an effort to cope with ever increasing passenger numbers availing of the direct route from Ireland to France Irish Continental decided to lengthen the *Saint Killian*. Entering dry dock in Amsterdam on 12 November 1981 she emerged 15 weeks later some 31.85 metres longer and renamed *Saint Killian II*. The project cost IR£7.5m and provided accommodation for an additional 517 passengers and 98 cars. Early in 1994, following a mishap with the *Isle of Innisfree (I)* and her berth at Holyhead the *Saint Killian II* operated a Dublin–Liverpool freight service and, during the international rugby weekend, some passenger runs from Dublin to Pembroke Dock were also made.

Author's collection

In 1987 the *Saint Patrick II* almost became a full-time Belfast Car Ferries unit when she was earmarked as a replacement for the *Saint Colum 1* on the sister company's route from Belfast to Liverpool. In the event the 'Paddy' returned to Rosslare in spring 1988 and she is seen here arriving at Le Havre in July of that year. (See also *City of Cork*, page 32)

Author

During the winter months the *Saint Patrick II* often found herself on charter to other operators, most notably North Sea Ferries, Tallink, P&O European Ferries and Sealink British Ferries. A regular charter was to B+I Line and on 6 January 1984 the *Saint Patrick II* carried out berthing trials at Holyhead prior to taking up the Dublin–Liverpool/Holyhead service while the *Leinster* and *Connacht* were overhauled. In this early 1989 view she is arriving at Rosslare wearing B&I Line funnel colours while on charter to cover the company's fleet overhaul program. The 'Paddy' finally left the fleet upon the arrival of the *Normandy* and is today in service in Canadian waters as the *CTMA Vacancier*.

Brian Cleare

The handsome *Scottish Coast* of 1956 operated the then seasonal service between Ardrossan and Belfast from 1965 until the arrival of the purpose-built car ferry *Lion* in 1968. To provide for the increasing number of cars on offer the passenger ship was fitted with a temporary ramp and lift in her forward well deck to enable up to 25 cars to be driven on and off. She also acted as relief on the Belfast–Liverpool run for the *Ulster Prince* and *Ulster Queen* during their first overhauls. *Richard Danielson Library*

The *Seacat Danmark* arrives off Liverpool's Pier Head from Douglas in July 1998. During the previous winter the 74 metre craft had operated between Stranraer and Belfast during *SeaCat Scotland*'s annual overhaul. Transferred to the Isle of Man routes for the 1998 season she was used to reopen passenger services between Heysham and Belfast in 1999. She returned to English Channel operation in 2000 before moving away to Italy in 2004 as the *Pescara Jet*. *Author*

In 1994 the Isle of Man Steam Packet Co chartered *SeaCat Boulogne* from Sea Containers. Renamed *SeaCat Isle of Man* she took up service on 28 June 1994. The following winter was spent operating on sub-charter between Stranraer and Belfast before spending time with Condor Ferries on the English Channel. *SeaCat Isle of Man* was a huge success but she was returned to the lessors at the end of the season and the Isle of Man was without a fast craft in 1996. In this view *SeaCat Isle of Man,* under the command of Capt Vernon Kinley, is arriving at Dun Laoghaire for berthing trials on 21 May 1997. Following the purchase of the Steam Packet by Sea Containers fast craft services were quickly reintroduced and *SeaCat Isle of Man* returned to the fold. Apart from spending the 1998 season on the English Channel the craft has remained on the Irish Sea ever since. By the end of the 2004 season speculation was mounting that the vessel had reached the end of its Irish Sea career.   *Paddy Cahill*

With Hobart's Mount Wellington as the backdrop a new *SeaCat Scotland* is seen during trials in Tasmania before introducing high speed car ferry services on the Irish Sea on 1 June 1992 when she inaugurated the Stranraer–Belfast service.   *Author's collection*

In 1999 *SeaCat Scotland* opened an additional service to Troon and such was its success that Stranraer was dropped from 2000. Replaced by the larger *Rapide* in 2002, *SeaCat Scotland* was transferred to the English Channel.   *Author*

Opposite top: The French Sealink ferry *Senlac* approaches Rosslare on 2 July 1987. The ship was chartered by B&I Line as their contribution to the joint service Fishguard–Rosslare route for the 1987 season. At one point B&I considered purchasing the former Newhaven–Dieppe ship but in the event she was sold for further service in Greek waters. The *Senlac* had previously ventured into the Irish Sea during the mid-1980s when she was overhauled at Holyhead's marine workshops. The author sailed on the ship from Paros to Piræus in August 2000 and was surprised to find she was very much the 'old' *Senlac*. Summer 2004 saw her operate as the *Express Apollon* out of Rafina to Mykonos.   *Brian Cleare*

Opposite bottom: Until the availability of the new *Holyhead Ferry 1* in 1966 the Dover train ferry *Shepperton Ferry*, provided overhaul relief to the *Caledonian Princess* on the Stranraer–Larne crossing. A sister of the *Hampton Ferry*, she made her first appearance on the route in April 1962. Her final spell on the North Channel was between 15 February and 13 March 1965. The stalwart ship remained in service between Dover and Dunkerque until 1972 when she was sold for breaking up in Spain.   *Brian Cleare collection*

Built by Harland & Wolff at Belfast for the Dover–Calais flagship service in 1980, the *St Anselm* was diverted to Fishguard in March 1983 while en route to Dover from Belfast following a major refit by her builders. A recurring engine problem with the *Stena Normandica* on 27 March forced a withdrawal from service but fortunately the 'Anselm' was available to maintain the Rosslare link for two days while repairs were carried out. (See also *Stena Cambria*, page 127)   *Brian Cleare collection*

On 15 April 1985 Sealink British Ferries purchased their chartered *Stena Normandica* (see page 140) for continuing service on the Fishguard Rosslare route. The ship had been hugely successful since her introduction on the link in 1979 and in keeping with her popularity she took the name *St Brendan* from the Irish Saint renowned for his navigational exploits. *Gary Davies/Maritime Photographic*

Opposite top: Not so popular was a move by Sealink British Ferries and B&I Line to rationalise sailings on the Irish Sea. A pooling arrangement was established and after two uneasy seasons the *St Brendan* returned to service, after overhaul, on 4 February 1987 sporting a new joint service livery, displaying the names of both operators. Hideous to say the least there was much relief when the partnership ended and the *St Brendan* returned from her 1988 overhaul once again resplendent in full Sealink colours. At 2140 on 4 March 1990 the *St Brendan* departed Rosslare for the last time. In the ten years since she entered Irish Sea service she built traffic on the route to a level where she had become, quite simply, too small. Under her new name, *Moby Vincent*, she left Fishguard bound for Italy, and a new career, three days later. *Sean Martley*

The brand new *St Christopher* arrives at Rosslare on 20 March 1981. Destined for the Dover–Calais service the new ship was to make her maiden voyage between Fishguard and Rosslare thereby allowing the *Stena Normandica* to stand down for overhaul. The 'Christopher' duly arrived at Rosslare for berthing trials early on 15 March, but instead of proceeding to Fishguard to take up the run she instead returned northwards to Dun Laoghaire where she arrived in darkness for further ramp trials. She then crossed to Holyhead to operate her maiden voyage in place of the *St Columba* on 17 March. This complete, it was back south and she finally took up service at Fishguard with the afternoon sailing two days later. It was not until 13 April that Dover finally got its new ship. (See also *Stena Antrim*, page 125) *Jack Phelan*

Opposite top: The *St Columba*, probably the best known of all Sealink Irish Sea ferries, was ordered in March 1975 as an eventual replacement for the mail ships *Hibernia* and *Cambria* and the car ferry *Holyhead Ferry 1*. With accommodation for 2,400 passengers in two classes and space for up to 335 cars on the vehicle deck, the ship was a much needed breath of fresh air to the Holyhead–Dun Laoghaire service. On 27 April 1977, under the command of Capt Len Evans, the new ship sailed on her inaugural voyage to Dun Laoghaire with members of the Irish Government, British Rail Board and other VIPs on board. The following morning she returned to Holyhead after a blessing ceremony on Dun Laoghaire's Carlisle Pier. She entered service on 3 May. She is pictured here in October 1982 alongside Holyhead's Refit Berth, undergoing conversion to a one class ship. In March of that year the ship operated on the Fishguard–Rosslare service in lieu of the *Stena Normandica*, this being the first and only occasion, while under the Sealink flag, she operated away from the route for which she was built. (See also *Stena Adventurer (I)*, page 123 and *Stena Hibernia*, page 134)

Capt Neville Lester

Opposite bottom: *St Columba* is seen looking her best, in Sealink British Ferries livery, following a major rebuild in Bremerhaven in spring 1986. When the *St Columba* returned to service she boasted a new style of luxury and comfort that earned the ship quite an excellent reputation. By this time engine problems which dogged her early years had been ironed out and she proved to be a most reliable ship. Unfortunately her superb facilities were lost in 1991 when, as the *Stena Hibernia*, she was again restyled in line with the 'Travel Service Concept' of new owners Stena Line. At the end of January 1990 a fire broke out in the *St Columba*'s engine room on her inward sailing to Holyhead. With the ship disabled one hour off the Welsh coast and with winds reaching gale force, a distress call was sent out by Senior Master Capt John Bakewell. By the time the rescue services arrived the crew had managed to bring the blaze under control. The whole event, during which B&I Line's *Leinster* stood by, was marked by the absence of panic onboard, and a situation which was potentially extremely negative in fact drew nothing but commendations for the manner in which it was handled.

Author

Built in 1947 as a passenger ship for the Fishguard–Rosslare service the *St David (III)* was converted to a side loading car ferry in 1964 in response to growing demands for drive-on drive-off car capacity on the link. The move certainly improved matters but by 1966 car traffic had outgrown both the *St David* and *St Andrew*, the latter being a passenger-only ship capable of accommodating a small number of crane loaded cars. The arrival of the *Duke of Rothesay* in 1967 meant the *St David*'s days were numbered and at the end of the 1969 season she was transferred to Holyhead as relief steamer. She finished her Irish Sea days operating between Dun Laoghaire and Heysham in support of the mail ships *Hibernia* and *Cambria* following the Britannia Bridge disaster, which severed Anglesey's rail link with the mainland.

Brian Cleare collection

Opposite top: Originally planned for Sealink's Fishguard–Rosslare route, the *St David (IV)* was instead allocated to Holyhead as the second ship when it transpired the *Stena Normandica* was proving to be a major success on the southern route. The ship arrived at Holyhead on 5 August 1981, replacing the chartered *Prinsessan Desirée* in service five days later. At the end of her first season the *St David* replaced the *St Columba* as the route's main ship, the new vessel being more economical to operate. By early 1983 the roles had been reversed and the *St David* now spent her winter months relieving at other ports, including Stranraer and Fishguard. She is seen here from a laid-up *St Columba* in October 1982. (See also *Stena Caledonia*, page 126)

Capt Neville Lester

Opposite bottom: The *St David* displays her new Sealink British Ferries livery. Following a short-lived transfer to the English Channel the ship returned to the Irish Sea and the Stranraer–Larne route in January 1986, filling the void left by the departure of the *Antrim Princess* to the Isle of Man Steam Packet. Her final spell on the Holyhead–Dun Laoghaire service was in April 1988 when she relieved the *St Columba*. Unfortunately she suffered an engine room fire while alongside at the Irish port forcing an early withdrawal from service for repairs before she returned to the Scottish link. (See also *Stena Caledonia*, page 126)

Author's collection

The arrival of the HSS concept on the Holyhead–Dun Laoghaire service numbered the *Stena Hibernia*'s remaining days on the Irish Sea. Renamed *Stena Adventurer (I)* in January 1996, and repainted in full Stena Line livery, the ship was almost transferred to Dover where her high passenger capacity would have been welcomed. In the event she remained at Holyhead beyond the entry into service of the *Stena Explorer* on 10 April 1996. Having played support to the *Stena Explorer* during the summer season the end for the conventional ferry service finally came on 30 September 1996. The *Stena Adventurer* was laid up at Dun Laoghaire as the port of Holyhead could not offer a berth for the ship and for one month the former flagship of the Sealink Irish Sea fleet remained on standby in the event of mechanical problems on the HSS. Now carrying her third name, *Stena Adventurer* (previously *St Columba*, then *Stena Hibernia*) is seen at Belfast on 18 April 1997 with the *Stena Galloway* getting underway for Stranraer. Before being moved to Belfast for lay-up pending sale she was permitted one final visit to Holyhead, operating one round trip to clear a backlog of traffic on 29 October. The following evening, under the command of Capt Jim Wilcox, the *Stena Adventurer* slipped out of Dun Laoghaire for the last time. As she left the harbour Stena Line's port vehicles lined the quay sounding their horns. In response, the *Stena Adventurer*'s whistle echoed around Dun Laoghaire as she completed her final swing before heading into Dublin Bay. Eight hours later she arrived at Belfast, 'Finished with Engines' being rung off at 0240hrs on 31 October. It was not too long before the *Stena Adventurer* was required again and on 3 November she was pressed into service to Stranraer. Unfortunately one of her crossings took 16 hours as she sheltered off Larne in high seas. Her final commercial sailing under the Stena Line flag was from the Scottish port to Belfast at 0230hrs on 7 November under the command of Capt Peter Lockyer. On 9 May, renamed *Express Aphrodite*, she crossed her former Holyhead–Dun Laoghaire passage as she sailed south for the warmer climes of the Aegean. (See also *St Columba*, page 121 and *Stena Hibernia*, page 134)

Author

The impressive new *Stena Adventurer (II)* entered service between Holyhead and Dublin on 1 July 2003. Built by South Korean shipbuilder Hyundai Heavy Industries at a cost of £60m the new ship has greatly improved services to both passengers and freight customers alike, although early in 2004 it was not possible for foot passengers to travel on the ship.

Top: Gary Davies/Maritime Photographic
Bottom: Author

On 7 April 1991 Sealink Stena Line's *Stena Antrim* entered service on the Stranraer–Larne route. As the *St Christopher* (see page 119) she was the third ship in the quartet built by Harland & Wolff between 1980 and 1981 and her arrival on the North Channel saw three of the near-sisters reunited on one route. The *Stena Antrim* saw service between Dun Laoghaire and Holyhead in January 1995 while covering the overhaul period of sister *Stena Cambria*. Her stint at Holyhead complete the 'Antrim' then moved to Fishguard while the *Stena Felicity* was overhauled. On 11 November the *Stena Antrim* operated the last sailing from Larne to Stranraer, ending a link lasting more than 123 years. The following day saw the opening of the new Belfast–Stranraer operation. March 1998 saw the removal of the *Stena Antrim* to the English Channel and the Newhaven–Dieppe run. The following month she was withdrawn from service and after two months laid up at Zeebrugge she was sold for service between Algeciras and Tangier as the *Ibn Batouta*. The *Stena Antrim* is seen here leaving Belfast for Stranraer in July 1996.   *Author*

When Stena Line acquired Sealink British Ferries the *St David* (see page 123) was renamed *Stena Caledonia* with port of registry changing from London to Stranraer. She is seen here leaving Larne for her home port during the summer of 1992.   *Author*

The *Stena Caledonia* sails down Loch Ryan en route to Belfast in July 1999. Twelve months previously, on 13 July 1998, she operated a sailing between Rosslare and Roscoff as one of three Stena ships chartered to assist with the movement of equipment following the Irish leg of the Tour de France cycle race. The last of the Harland & Wolff 'Saint class' ships to remain in service in UK waters, and indeed the last Sealink ship to remain in service with Stena Line, she continues in service alongside the HSS *Stena Voyager*. However her days are very much numbered.

Author

Built as the *St Anselm* (see page 117), *Stena Cambria* was transferred to Holyhead as a second ship to partner the *Stena Hibernia* but soon after her arrival in February 1991 she blotted her copybook when she touched the bottom of the Welsh port's Inner Harbour. After a stint back at Dover the 'Cambria' finally re-entered service at Holyhead on 8 July. In this scene the *Stena Cambria* passes sister ship *Stena Antrim* in Dublin Bay in January 1995. The Stranraer ship was operating relief sailings and she is actually on the *Stena Cambria*'s scheduled roster while the 'Cambria' is on the *Stena Hibernia*'s slot. On 11 November, the 'Cambria' operated the final Stranraer–Larne crossing before the Irish terminal moved to Belfast.

Author

Leaving Dublin Port for Holyhead while covering for the *Stena Challenger* in March 1998 is the *Stena Cambria*. Devoid of Stena Line markings in readiness for a transfer to the newly merged P&O Stena Line at Dover, the 'Cambria' had been hastily called back for a final Irish Sea stint in January when the relief ship *Stena Caledonia* was unexpectedly taken off the Fishguard–Rosslare route.

Paddy Cahill

The *Stena Challenger* leaves Dublin for Holyhead in December 1996. The arrival of the ship on the freight service three months previously opened the fledgling route to passengers thanks to her ability to accommodate up to 500 persons. This ability proved its worth during the winter months when adverse weather affected HSS sailings on the Dun Laoghaire run. The *Stena Challenger* remained at Holyhead until her sale to Canadian operators in April 2001.

Author

Stena Line's *Stena Europe* leaves Rosslare for Fishguard on 15 September 2003. Entering service on the crossing on 13 March 2002 after a £4.5m major refit the 'Europe' replaced the *Koningin Beatrix* which then transferred to the Karlskrona–Gdynia service as *Stena Baltica*. In January 2003 the 'Europe' hit the news when she lost power near Tuskar Rock, just off the Irish coast. Five helicopters were scrambled to winch 155 passengers to safety, but the rescue was aborted as engineers brought the ship back under her own power. Since then the *Stena Europe* has settled down to become a very popular addition to the Irish Sea fleet. Coincidentally the ship now shares Rosslare with her sister ship *Normandy*, now operating with Irish Ferries. The *Normandy* was once Sealink's *St Nicholas*, built as the *Prinsessan Birgitta* and taken over by Stena for the charter market. *Stena Europe* was built as the *Kronprinsessan Victoria*.   *Author*

Opposite: The new HSS for Stena Line's Hook of Holland to Harwich service, *Stena Discovery*, actually operated her maiden voyage on 26 April 1997 while relieving the *Stena Voyager* on the Stranraer–Belfast service. The craft remained on the North Channel until 24 May. Although she has not since operated on an Irish Sea route she is a regular visitor to these waters by virtue of her annual overhauls at the Belfast yard of Harland & Wolff.   *Gary Davies/Maritime Photographic*

This photograph shows the first arrival of the HSS *Stena Explorer* in Dun Laoghaire Harbour for berthing trials on 31 March 1996. Under the command of Capt John Roberts the craft left Dun Laoghaire for Holyhead at 0653 on 10 April on her historic maiden commercial voyage, heralding a new era of Irish Sea ferry operations. Her second sailing from the Irish port that day saw some 1109 passengers and 230 cars loaded over the specially designed linkspan in little over ten minutes. With her four GE gas turbines providing a service speed of 40 knots the *Stena Explorer* was able to operate up to five round trips daily, each with a crossing time of just 99 minutes. As with any new technology there can be teething troubles and it must be said the *Stena Explorer* had her fair share of these. Her first two seasons were plagued with cancelled sailings but one by one the technical problems have been largely overcome. On one occasion she was holed above and below the waterline when a fender she contacted failed while going alongside at Dun Laoghaire. Depending on the time of the year she now operates anything between two and four round trips daily, her thirsty gas turbine engines being a factor in the move to consolidate sailings.   *Author*

Breaking away from the linkspan the *Stena Explorer* powers away from her Dun Laoghaire berth. As with all fast ferry services, fast port turnarounds are essential. Through multi-lane loading and discharge the 1500-passenger HSS is capable of handling 350 cars or 50 trucks and 110 cars on and off in approximately 30 minutes. The *Stena Explorer* normally provides overhaul relief for sister HSS *Stena Voyager* on the Stranraer–Belfast service.   *Author*

Renamed and displaying the modified Sealink Stena Line livery, the *Stena Felicity* rounds the end of Rosslare Pier in 1992.
(See also *Felicity*, page 51)   *Author*

Dwarfing the rival *Isle of Inishmore (I)* at Rosslare the *Stena Felicity* pulls away on a 0900 sailing to Fishguard in September 1996. The *Stena Felicity*'s last passenger sailing under the Stena flag was on 3 July 1997. Sailing to Pembroke to allow her replacement, the *Koningin Beatrix*, onto the ramp at Fishguard, the ship arrived alongside at 1720hrs. After discharge and destoring she left for Bremerhaven where she was returned to her owners. Considered by many to be the finest ship to ever sail on the Fishguard–Rosslare run, the 'Felicity' truly did bring a new level of travel to Irish waters.   *Author*

Replacing the *Stena Challenger* on the Holyhead–Dublin service in April 2001 was the chartered Italian-flag *Stena Forwarder*. The ship was another boost for the service which started in 1995 as a freight only operation. With accommodation for 1000 passengers, 500 more than her predecessor, the *Stena Forwarder* also increased freight capacity by some 60%. With the arrival of the new *Stena Adventurer* in sight, the 'Fowarder' was sold by her owners for service in Mexico. Her final sailing from Dublin was on 13 April 2003, by which time she had already been renamed *California Star*.

Gary Davies/Maritime Photographic

Opposite bottom: Stranraer's *Stena Galloway* swings in Dun Laoghaire Harbour before going astern onto St Michael's Pier on 24 July 1992. A gearbox failure in the *Stena Cambria* had sent the Scottish ship south the previous day for her first spell of service away from the route for which she was built. It was not a particularly happy time for the ship. Her bulbous bow prevented her from berthing bow in at the Irish port forcing her operation as a stern loader. As time passed the *Stena Galloway* increasingly fell behind schedule as most trucks had to be reversed on board and foot passengers had to disembark over the vehicle deck. The 'Cambria' finally returned to service on 21 August allowing the *Stena Galloway* to return to home waters. (See also *Galloway Princess*, page 54)   *Author*

On a still morning in August 1996 the *Stena Galloway* is seen approaching Belfast. The arrival of the HSS *Stena Voyager* on the Stranraer–Belfast route in July 1996 primarily reduced the *Stena Galloway* to freight operations, her full passenger facilities only being used on peak sailings and during HSS cancellations. On 11 September 2001 she entered service on the Fishguard–Rosslare service, following a mishap when the *Koningin Beatrix* was berthing at the Irish port. Just as she had done at Holyhead in 1992 the *Stena Galloway* proved totally unsuitable for the southern route, a hoistable ramp having to be used to connect the shore ramp to the ships stern. Again long delays ensued as it became very clear she could not cope with all the traffic on offer, however she remained on the crossing until 28 October when the 'KB' finally returned to service. On 8 February 2002 the *Stena Galloway* made a surprise visit to Liverpool for a pre-sale hull inspection for potential new owners. On 22 February she completed service on the North Channel and renamed *Le Rif*, under the Moroccan flag, for new owners IMTC, she sailed from Belfast for the last time late the following evening.   *Sam Somerville*

Probably one of the most attractive looking ferries to sail in Irish waters was the *Stena Germanica*, on charter to B+I Line for the Cork to Swansea service in 1978. The ship went on to endure a somewhat varied career which included operation as an accommodation ship for oil workers. After striking a reef off Puerto Rico in 1985 she was broken up on site. *Author's collection*

The *St Columba* (see page 121), by now re-named *Stena Hibernia* (and later *Stena Adventurer*, see page 123), leaves Dun Laoghaire on 14 March 1991 on her first eastbound sailing following an £8m rebuild in Germany. As the first ship to introduce Stena Line's 'Travel Service Concept' to the Sealink fleet the *Stena Hibernia* re-entered service with an á la carte restaurant, a self-service restaurant and pizza factory, a Show Bar with "resident band and visiting cabaret", an Irish Bar with traditional Irish music, a Business Club and Conference Centre, casino and various lounges. *Author*

Bow in at Dun Laoghaire on 9 January 1992, in poor light and drizzle, is the *Stena Hengist*. The ship operated one round trip per day while the *Stena Cambria*, followed by *Stena Hibernia*, underwent their annual overhauls. Released from Holyhead the ship then moved to the Stranraer–Larne run while each of the ships there were overhauled. On 14 March the *Stena Hengist* operated her last sailing under the Sealink flag. (See also *Hengist*, page 56)

Author

Opposite top: En route to Folkestone from overhaul at Birkenhead the *Stena Horsa* was diverted to Holyhead on 12 February 1991 when the *Stena Cambria* was withdrawn for emergency dry docking. The ship made two round trips to Dun Laoghaire before continuing on her voyage south. Closing the Folkestone–Boulogne service on 31 December 1992 the ship was withdrawn and laid-up, pending sale, at Milford Haven. Sold for further service in Greece, 2004 saw her in operation as the *Penelope A* on Agoudimos Lines Rafina–Andros–Tinos–Mykonos run. (See also Horsa, page 59)

Gary Davies/Maritime Photographic

Opposite bottom: The *Stena Invicta* is pictured alongside at Dublin in December 1999. The P&O Stena Line ferry was chartered to Stena Line for overhaul relief at Holyhead and Fishguard before being handed over to new owners Color Line after her last sailing from Rosslare on 20 March 2000.

Author

A stranger in the camp during spring 1996 was the Newhaven–Dieppe ferry *Stena Londoner*, seen here breaking away from Dun Laoghaire's Carlisle Pier for Holyhead on 5 April. Fresh from Fishguard where she had operated the Rosslare run while the *Stena Felicity* was overhauled, the ship was pressed into service at Holyhead following delays with the entry into service of the HSS *Stena Explorer*. Returned to her French owners by Stena Line in June 1996 the ship was renamed *SeaFrance Monet* for service between Calais and Dover. Sold to Spanish operator Armas in May 2000 the ship continues in service in the Canary Islands as the *Volcan de Tacande*.

Author

In February 1998 *Stena Lynx* (formerly *Stena Sea Lynx*, see page 141) briefly saw service on the Stranraer–Belfast service. Her charter to Stena Line expired at the end of the following summer season and today the craft operates in Korean waters.   *Author*

Originally acquired for service between Dover and Calais in 1996, the 81 metre Incat catamaran *Stena Lynx III* was transferred to the Fishguard–Rosslare service in December 1998. Her first task on the Irish Sea was to provide overhaul relief for the *Stena Explorer* on the Holyhead–Dun Laoghaire route. Upon the return of the HSS the *Stena Lynx III* then sailed north to Stranraer for a brief period in service on the Belfast run before returning to Fishguard in time to open the fast craft season. On completion of her charter at the end of the 2003 season Stena Line concluded outright purchase of the craft, ensuring her continued service at Fishguard in 2004.   *PP Young*

This view shows the chartered *Stena Nordica (I)* on passage from Stranraer to Larne in the late 1960s. Chartered to operate alongside the *Caledonian Princess* pending delivery of the new *Antrim Princess* in 1967, the Swedish-flagged ship entered service from Larne on 14 February 1966. Although she was considerably smaller than the *Caledonian Princess* she was hugely popular, particularly with British Rail's freight customers. In the event the *Stena Nordica* was retained on the route until 27 March 1971. For one week in October 1970 she operated between Belfast and Ardrossan on charter to Burns & Laird. She visited Ardrossan again during her last month in service with British Rail following technical problems with the linkspan at Stranraer. Sold for further service in Venezuela in 1975 the ship was gutted by fire on 7 May 1980.

Ian Collard

On 4 and 5 September 1978 the Stena Line ferry *Stena Nordica (II)* carried out berthing trials at Fishguard and Rosslare leading to the belief that Sealink were going to acquire her to replace the *Avalon*. In the event the company instead chartered her sister *Stena Normandica*. The 'Nordica' did see service at Fishguard in February 1980 and she is seen here on the passenger berth while a freshly overhauled *Stena Normandica* lies astern before resuming sailings to Rosslare.

Brian Cleare collection

On charter to B+I Line the *Stena Nordica (II)* arrives at Rosslare from Pembroke on 20 March 1981. Entering service with the Irish company on 16 October 1980 a series of breakdowns plagued the ship and two months later she had to retire to Verolme Cork Dockyard for attention. Lacking stabilisers and other enhancements benefiting her sister on the rival Sealink service, the *Stena Nordica* was not a success for B+I and she was finally returned to Stena Line in May 1981.

Jack Phelan

This view shows Sealink's chartered *Stena Normandica* alongside at Rosslare in May 1979. Entering service between Fishguard and Rosslare on 2 April 1979 the *Stena Normandica* was originally taken on charter pending delivery of the new *St David* from Harland & Wolff. Such was the early success of the Swedish-flagged ship that it was decided the send the 'David' to Holyhead instead and retain the 'Normandica' on the Irish Sea. An overnight boom in traffic was recorded but this was brought to an abrupt halt in June when she suffered major engine trouble. In a freight only role she continued to operate on one engine until 23 July when she was withdrawn for repairs at Holyhead. Two months passed before the *Stena Normandica* returned to Fishguard but she soon settled back into service and went on to become a ship much liked by passengers and crew alike. In April 1985 she was purchased by Sealink and renamed *St Brendan* (see page 118). *Brian Cleare collection*

Stena Line's fast ferry pioneer, the 74 metre *Stena Sea Lynx*, arrives in Dun Laoghaire for berthing trials prior to entering service on the Holyhead service. During her first six months in service the total market on the service grew by over 200,000 passengers and 40,000 cars. With capacity for 425 passengers and 80 cars the *Stena Sea Lynx* cut the three hours 30 minutes crossing time to just one hour 50 minutes. Her immediate success led to the acquisition of the larger *Stena Sea Lynx II* and on 26 June 1994 the *Stena Sea Lynx* arrived at Fishguard to introduce high speed sailings to the southern route. (See also *Stena Lynx*, page 138)   *Author*

The *Stena Sea Lynx II* is seen in Dublin Bay in this 1995 view. Under the command of Capt Hugh Farrell the craft operated her maiden commercial voyage between Holyhead and Dun Laoghaire on 22 June 1994, replacing the smaller *Stena Sea Lynx*. To reflect Stena Line's dropping of the Sealink brand name, in February 1996 the craft was renamed *Stena Lynx II* and transferred to the English Channel.

Author

Swansea Cork Ferries' *Superferry* clears Cork Harbour outward bound for Swansea. Following the sale of Swansea Cork Ferries to Strintzis Lines of Greece at the end of 1992 the Greek-flagged *Superferry* was introduced onto the run on 5 March 1993. When Swansea Cork Ferries was sold early in 2000 the *Superferry* remained on charter to the new owners for one more season before returning to service in the Aegean. *Author*

Opposite: On 21 July 1996 Stranraer–Belfast became the second Stena Line service to receive a HSS craft. Like her Holyhead sister *Stena Explorer*, the *Stena Voyager* also experienced early teething problems but as time went by these were gradually ironed out. In March 1997 she operated on the Holyhead–Dun Laoghaire run while the *Stena Explorer* received her first overhaul. Damage to her North Sea sister *Stena Discovery* saw the *Stena Voyager* temporarily transferred to the Harwich–Hook of Holland service from 22 January until 4 April 1998, causing much outcry on both sides of the North Channel. In this view, captured by Gary Andrews on 5 January 2001, the *Stena Voyager* is seen leaving Larne for Belfast. The craft had berthed at the port's Curran Quay for several hours to allow an underwater survey to take place.   *Gary Andrews*

On 8 April 2002 the *Superferry* returned to the Cork–Swansea route having been purchased by the company's new owners, Briarstar Ltd.

Jack Phelan

The monohull fast craft *SuperSeaCat Two* swings in Dun Laoghaire harbour on 9 March 1998 prior to commencing service on Sea Containers' Liverpool–Dublin service three days later. Her first year on the route was plagued with technical problems and poor weather, resulting in many cancelled sailings and much bad press on both sides of the Irish Sea. In 1998 she was removed to the English Channel but returned to the Irish Sea in 2000 to operate on the seasonal service between Heysham and Belfast. On this occasion she proved to be more reliable, that is until the end of the season when the route was terminated earlier than scheduled due to continuing problems with the craft. Transferred to the English Channel for 2001, she spent all of 2002 laid up at Portsmouth before undergoing major engine works and a return to the Irish Sea on the Liverpool–Dublin/Douglas routes in March 2003. Under the flag of the Isle of Man Steam Packet the *SuperSeaCat Two* has since performed better than any year since 1998.

Paddy Cahill

P&O's *SuperStar Express* is seen arriving at Larne in May 2003. Making her maiden voyage on the North Channel on 18 April 2000 the *SuperStar Express,* a former Portsmouth vessel, brought much needed reliability to P&O's fast craft service following the troubled *Jetliner* years. Despite the arrival of the new *European Highlander* P&O decided to continue a charter for the craft and after winter lay-up she returned to service in 2002 and again in 2003 when she also served Troon in addition to her Cairnryan sailings. Following a very successful first season on the Troon–Larne route, P&O Irish Sea continued to operate the vessel until September 2004, although following changes announced by P&O the following month she was returned off charter and replaced at Larne by another former Portsmouth vessel, the *Cherbourg Express.*

Norman Johnston

Opposite: Replacing the *SuperSeaCat Two* on the Liverpool–Dublin service in 1999 was sister ship *SuperSeaCat Three*. An improved version of the earlier craft, a twin bow thrust and enhanced ride control system provided a more reliable service between the two cities. With the loss of duty free sales, the Dublin service was dropped to one round trip daily during the summer season, in favour of an additional round trip from Liverpool to Douglas. The craft was replaced in 2001 by the Incat 81 metre craft *Rapide*.

Author

Brittany Ferries' *Tregastel* rests at Cork's Ringaskiddy terminal before a sailing to Roscoff in October 1985.

Jack Phelan

Opposite: In February 1989 B&I Line were forced to charter tonnage to maintain their services during the annual overhaul period. Sally Line's *The Viking* could not be considered a success and even before she entered service between Dublin and Holyhead she broke down, delaying the Leinster's overhaul by one week. On 14 February two round trips were lost due to bow visor trouble and one week later she failed while occupying Holyhead's station berth forcing a hasty shift to the port's container terminal to allow the incoming *St Columba* to berth.

Gary Davies/Maritime Photographic

The Isle of Man Steam Packet's chartered *Tynwald* (ex *Antrim Princess*, see page 24) arrives at Douglas from Heysham on 6 June 1989. With the introduction of new safety standards following the loss of the *Herald of Free Enterprise* at Zeebrugge in 1987 the *Tynwald*'s days were numbered. Completing her final sailing on 18 February 1990 she was returned to her owners who promptly sold her for further service with Italy's Lauro Line.

John Hollingworth

The Belfast Steamship Co's handsome *Ulster Prince* sails down the River Lagan outbound for Liverpool early in her career. Both she and her sister were admired for their attractive lines but unfortunately from day one they were both outdated when compared with British Rail's new *Antrim Princess* at Stranraer. When the end came in November 1981 the ship sailed for lay-up at Ostend pending sale. She was finally sold in August 1982 for service in Greek waters. After a somewhat varied career she found herself operating between Port Rashid and the Iraqi port of Umm Qasr in 2001. *Richard Danielson Library*

Towards the end of her career the *Ulster Queen* was adorned in P&O Ferries livery. She too was sent to Ostend for lay up following the closure of the Belfast–Liverpool service but she was not idle for as long as the 'Prince', being sold to Cypriot owners in April 1982. *Richard Danielson Library*

A proud day for Irish Ferries as their new *Ulysses* enters Dublin Port for the first time on 4 March 2001. The ship, in its scale, its grandeur and its technical specifications, set new standards for the construction of passenger ferries in the 21st century. She is named in honour of James Joyce's 'Ulysses', the book that immortalised the life of Dublin on 16 June 1904. Built in the shipyard of Aker Finnyards in Rauma, Finland, at a total cost of €100 million, she stands 12 decks high and towers over other vessels at a height of 51 metres from keel to mast. With almost three miles of parking space for 1342 cars or 240 articulated trucks per sailing no other passenger car ferry in the world can match her vehicle carrying capacity. *Author*

Two very different concepts in Irish Sea travel! The HSS *Stena Explorer* passes Irish Ferries' *Ulysses* off the end of Holyhead breakwater. The Irish ship entered service on 25 March 2001 and in her first two years of operation lost only one round trip, that being due to teething problems. In February 2003, in order to keep operational following berth damage at Holyhead, the ship operated a freight-only service to Birkenhead. One word is sufficient to describe this ship – magnificent! How this scene has changed in the 20 years since the *Connacht* and *St David* met off Holyhead. *Gary Davies/Maritime Photographic*

Above: The splendid *Val de Loire* of Brittany Ferries is alongside at Roscoff after an overnight crossing from Cork in June 1998. *Author*

Opposite top: A short-lived venture in July 1999 was St Malo Cork Ferries, operated by the *Venus* on charter from Greek operator Ventouris Ferries. Managed by Swansea Cork Ferries the service was established to primarily meet the needs of the Irish agriculture industry but other traffic was also accepted. Sailing three times a week the *Venus* offered capacity for up to 80 lorries in addition to cars and 300 passengers. Dry goods, general commercial traffic and holiday traffic were expected to account for a large share of bookings but the service was closed after just four months. *Jack Phelan*

Opposite bottom: On charter to Sealink Manx Line, Townsend Thoresen's *Viking III* storms out of Douglas into the teeth of an Irish Sea gale on 23 March 1980. Having finished her Isle of Man charter on 31 March the *Viking III* was soon back in the Irish Sea, this time on charter to B+I Line. On 23 May 1980 she opened the company's new Rosslare–Pembroke service, continuing to operate on the link until her charter expired on 27 September. Engine trouble on the *Manx Viking* saw an immediate return to the Isle of Man where she remained until 15 October. *Richard Danielson*

Following the departure of relief vessel *Earl Godwin* Townsend Thoresen's *Viking Victory* was briefly chartered by Sealink Manx Line from 9 April 1981 to cover Heysham–Douglas sailings until the return of the *Manx Viking*.
Stan Basnett

Townsend Thoresen's Portsmouth–Cherbourg ferry *Viking Viscount* was a visitor to the North Channel in March 1988 providing overhaul relief on the Cairnryan service. She is seen here at Portsmouth shortly before her Irish Sea stint and displaying an intermediate livery folllowing the sale of Townsend Thoresen to P&O. The vessel returned again in 1989 just prior to being renamed *Pride of Winchester*.

Author's collection

The *Villandry*, of Sealink's French partner SNCF, is pictured arriving at Douglas from Heysham while on charter in lieu of the *Manx Viking* in June 1983. This was not the ship's first visit to the Irish Sea, as for six weeks from 7 June 1982 she operated on the Stranraer–Larne crossing while the *Darnia* was being modified to carry more passengers. Having returned to the English Channel the *Villandry* was once again called to the Irish Sea when at the height of the season the *St Columba* suffered an engine failure. Having been laid up at a coal berth in Calais the ship was somewhat the worse for wear when she arrived at Holyhead late on 7 August. With the *St Columba* still struggling back and forth on one engine a major clean-up operation was underway on the Frenchman and it was not until the afternoon of 9 August that she sailed to Dun Laoghaire. The *St Columba* returned two days later but all was not well and on 12 August the *Villandry* was pressed back into service for a further three days. She was an interesting ship, affectionately known on the run as the 'Vile and Dry'!

Richard Danielson

In this view we see the *Vortigern* awaiting her 0900 sailing from Rosslare to Fishguard on 29 January 1987. The failure of B&I Line to provide a relief vessel for the joint service Fishguard operation during the overhaul of the *St Brendan* forced Sealink to bring the Folkestone-based *Vortigern* around for her first spell on the Irish Sea. A poor replacement for the 'Brendan' the 1969-built ship remained on the link until 4 February, by which time it was being suggested that she might be retained as a second peak season ferry. In the event B&I instead chartered the *Senlac* from SNCF and the *Vortigern* returned to the Dover Strait.

Brian Cleare

The *Vortigern* is seen at Holyhead's Refit Berth during her last week in Sealink service before sailing for Piræus and a new career in warmer climes. Having been laid up at Chatham in Kent pending disposal, the ship was reactivated for operation on the Holyhead–Dun Laoghaire freight service on 7 March 1987 following an engine failure in the cargo-only *Stena Sailer*. Arriving at the Welsh port two days later the ship made her first crossing to Dun Laoghaire on 10 March. She was deprived of the opportunity to operate on the passenger service and after the 0215 sailing to Dun Laoghaire on 31 March she returned to Holyhead in ballast for handing over to her new Greek owners. As the *Nisos Limnos* the ship was sold in September 2004, for breaking up in India, although she remained in service until the end of October. Demolition work on the former *Vortigern* began in mid-November.

Author

Memorable Moments

The *St David* Blockade

The announcement of B+I Line's intention to open a new route between Dublin and Holyhead in March 1982 provoked an angry response from the Welsh side of the Irish Sea. Port workers at Holyhead, fearful for their livelihoods, immediately refused to handle the B+I ship, threatening to "line the quays" if she appeared off the port. Appear she did, on 28 February, and having been met by a blockade of small boats across the mouth of the inner harbour she was forced to return to Dublin having failed in her attempts to carry out berthing trials.

On 2 March the inaugural commercial sailing was cancelled as attempts to break the deadlock commenced but by 8 March progress had still not been made and with B+I determined to open their new route the *Connacht* once again sailed for Holyhead. On arrival off the port she was again faced with the full fury of port workers and after an hour and a half waiting outside Captain Frank Devaney had no alternative but to return to Dublin.

The repeated failure of their ships to berth at Holyhead led B+I crews to take retaliatory action. While the *Connacht* was returning to Dublin a crew boarded the laid-up *Munster* and sailed her across Dublin Bay to Dun Laoghaire where she dropped anchor in the mouth of the harbour. Her intentions were to prevent access to any Sealink vessel. With a one hour 30 minutes head start over the returning *Connacht*, Sealink's *St David* approached Dublin Bay at 1800 to find her way into the harbour well and truly blocked.

I can well recall this most incredible sight. Seeing the *Munster* sailing across Dublin Bay towards Dun Laoghaire was unusual in itself, but to then watch as she slowed and manoeuvred across the mouth of the harbour seemed quite surreal.

On the bridge of the approaching *St David* there was a similar feeling as Captain Idwal Pritchard looked at ways of getting his ship into Dun Laoghaire. Calling the *Munster* by VHF radio to ask of their intentions Captain Pritchard was initially met with silence but the Irish ship eventually indicated they would not be moving. Asking if the *Munster* was anchored the *St David* was given a blunt "Yes."

Then followed the first of several attempts to break the blockade. The *St David* went for a gap between the *Munster*'s bow and the East Pier lighthouse, prompting a warning from the *Munster*'s Master that small boats were placed between his ship and the wall. The *St David* moved astern and coming to rest about a ship's length from the anchored vessel. She then made another run for a gap between the *Munster*'s stern and the West Pier but, using her engines, the B+I ship moved to block the ship again. Still the *St David*

Head to head
St David squares up to *Munster* in the mouth of Dun Laoghaire harbour.
Author's collection

continued her approach, finally coming to a halt seemingly within a few feet of the *Munster*. After a few breath taking moments the *St David* again moved astern. A highly manoeuvrable vessel, Captain Pritchard had full command of his ship and was able to do exactly what he wanted with her.

This game of cat and mouse continued for well over an hour, but each time the *Munster* thwarted the British ship's attempts. Finally, shortly before midnight the *St David* returned to Holyhead for stores and a reappraisal of the situation.

The following morning the *St David* reappeared off Dun Laoghaire once again finding the *Munster* firmly blockading the harbour. However, by now the Sealink ferry had an unwell passenger on board and following a doctor's call for medical treatment the *Munster* moved aside on humanitarian grounds. The *St David* quickly turned around and sailed again for Holyhead, and with all sailings suspended until further notice the B+I ship returned to her berth in Dublin.

No doubt such a spectacle will never be seen again.

The Bwana Swing

It was on a wild and wet day late in 1993 that I arrived in Holyhead for a winter crossing of the Irish Sea in the *Stena Hibernia,* in full expectation of a cancelled sailing. With winds gusting to southerly Force 9 the likelihood of the ship negotiating the bend in the inner harbour as she departed stern first was remote at best.

However to my surprise embarkation commenced, a sure sign that we were going to sail. Not wanting to get in the way I decided against approaching the bridge where a warm welcome was always waiting. Today, I thought, the Master will have enough on his plate just taking the ship out of Holyhead.

Stena Hibernia runs astern out of Holyhead's Inner Harbour.   *Author*

Under the command of Captain Ian Farrell the ship left the station berth and what followed next was quite remarkable, and had certainly never been attempted before.

For some months the *Stena Hibernia*'s Night Master, Captain Richard 'Bwana' Jones, had pondered the possibility of the 'Hibernia' being stuck on the station berth in a strong southerly gale, a condition that made leaving Holyhead stern first very difficult. Such an occurrence could keep the incoming *Stena Cambria* outside the port with no berth available until after the weather moderated and the *Stena Hibernia* departed. Poring over the charts Captain Jones felt it might just be possible to swing the ship within the confines of the inner harbour and proceed out through 'The Gut' bow first. A visit to the old container terminal further enforced his thinking that the manoeuvre could be done.

Captain Jones discussed the matter at length with the Day Master, Captain Farrell but there it rested until this very day when, in normal circumstances the sailing would have been postponed.

Captain Jones recalls:

> It was blowing a gale from the south, the Stena Sea Lynx *was cancelled and lying alongside the Refit berth, while the* Stena Cambria *was waiting off the breakwater. I was in bed as Ian was preparing for the afternoon sailing. The next thing I was rudely awakened and told I was required on the bridge. When I got there I was told, "This is your bloody idea so we'll do it together."*

Standing on the ship's after deck I could not believe my ears when I heard Captain Jones announce to the passengers that an attempt to swing the ship within the inner harbour was going to be made. At 129.2m long I was sure this was doomed to failure, the harbour being not much wider than the ship's length at its extreme points.

In a fine display of seamanship the *Stena Hibernia* moved down along the harbour and, with a line ashore aft, the stern was landed and pinned on a set of piles on the container terminal. The ship then canted around ever so gently, there being just enough space to clear forward.

Captain Jones continues:

> Lo and behold the 'Bwana Swing' was born and over time this method was much improved upon, but it could only be carried out if tidal conditions were right. The piles on the container berth were small and not just landing, but keeping the stern on them, was quite tricky.

Over many years I have witnessed many impressive acts of ship handling, particularly on a poor night at Dun Laoghaire in an easterly gale at low water, but that one occasion in Holyhead will forever remain firmly etched in my memory.

156

The ships and their routes

Name	Built	Passengers	Cars	Irish Sea Routes	Notes
Ailsa Princess	1971	1200	190	Stranraer–Larne 1971–1982/83, Holyhead–Dun Laoghaire, 1980/82, Douglas–Heysham, 1982.	
Antrim Princess	1967	1200	155	Stranraer–Larne 1967–1985, Holyhead–Dun Laoghaire, 1980 / 1982, Heysham–Douglas, 1980, 1981/82	
Armorique	1972	700	170	Roscoff–Cork, 1978–1982, Rosslare–Le Havre/Cherbourg, 1989/93, Belfast–Liverpool, 1989.	
Avalon	1963	1000	200	Fishguard–Rosslare, 1975–1978/79, Holyhead–Dun Laoghaire, 1976/77, 1979–1980.	
Ben-my-Chree (V)	1966	1400	70	Douglas–Liverpool & seasonal routes, 1966–1985	
Ben-my-Chree (VI)	1998	500	303	Douglas–Heysham, 1998–	
Benodet	1970	1200	260	Roscoff–Cork, 1984	
Bolette	1974	1200	300	Douglas–Holyhead, 1988	
Brave Merchant	1999	250	2000 lane metres	Liverpool–Dublin	
Bretagne	1989	2056	580	Roscoff–Cork, 1989–1992	
Caledonian Princess	1961	1400	103	Stranraer–Larne, 1961–1971, Fishguard–Rosslare, 1969/70/71–1975, Holyhead–Dun Laoghaire, 1968	
Celtic Pride	1972	1000	170	Swansea–Cork, 1987–1988, 1991–1992	
Channel Entente	1975	1000	220	Douglas–Heysham, 1990	ex-Saint Eloi
Chartres	1974	1400	240	Holyhead–Dun Laoghaire, 1994	
Cherbourg Express	1998	876	225	Larne–Cairnryan, 2004	
City of Cork	1973	1500	300	Swansea–Cork, 2001	ex-Saint Patrick II
Claymore	1978	500	47	Ardrossan–Douglas, 1994/95/96 Ballycastle–Campbeltown, 1997–1999	
Condor 10	1992	580	85	Fishguard–Rosslare	
Connacht	1979	1500	332	Cork–Swansea, 1979, Cork–Pembroke Dock, 1979–1980. Dublin–Liverpool, 1980–1988, Dublin–Holyhead, 1982–1988, Rosslare–Pembroke Dock, 1988–1988	
Cornouailles	1977	550	205	Roscoff–Cork, 1979/1980/1987	
Darnia	1977	412	255	Stranraer–Larne, 1978–1990, Fishguard–Rosslare, 1988, Holyhead–Dun Laoghaire 1980	

Name	Built	Passengers	Cars	Irish Sea Routes	Notes
Dawn Merchant	1999	250	2000 lane metres	Liverpool–Dublin, 1989–2001	
Diamant	1996	654	155	Liverpool–Dublin/Douglas, 2003	
Dover	1965	864	205	Holyhead–Dun Laoghaire, 1969–1976, Heysham–Dun Laoghaire, 1970/71, Fishguard–Rosslare, 1976	
Dragon	1967	850	250	Le Havre–Rosslare, 1969/70/71	
Duc de Normandie	1978	1535	350	Roscoff–Cork, 1992	
Duchesse Anne	1979	1300	290	Roscoff–Cork, 1993–1996, St Malo–Cork, 1993–1996	ex-*Connacht*
Duke of Argyll	1956	1400	105	Heysham–Belfast, 1970–1975, Holyhead–Dun Laoghaire, 1975	
Duke of Lancaster	1956	1400	105	Fishguard–Rosslare, 1975 / 1977, Holyhead–Dun Laoghaire, 1977–1978	
Duke of Rothesay	1956	1400	112	Fishguard–Rosslare, 1967–1972/73, Holyhead–Dun Laoghaire, 1973/74/75, Heysham–Belfast, 1973/74	
Earl Godwin	1966	928	170	Douglas–Heysham, 1981	
Earl Granville	1973	1200	233	Liverpool–Dun Laoghaire, 1988, Stranraer–Larne, 1990	
Earl Harold	1971	1800	190	Stranraer–Larne, 1985/86, Fishguard–Rosslare, 1988, Holyhead–Dun Laoghaire, 1988, Rosslare–Pembroke Dock, 1989	ex-*Ailsa Princess*
Earl Leofric	1965	725	205	Holyhead–Dun Laoghaire, 1978	ex-*Holyhead Ferry 1*
Earl Siward	1965	725	205	Holyhead–Dun Laoghaire, 1981	ex-*Dover*
Earl William	1964	500	180	Liverpool–Dun Laoghaire, 1988–1990. Holyhead–Dun Laoghaire, 1988 / 1990 / 1991	
European Ambassador	2000	405	375	Liverpool–Dublin, 2001. Mostyn–Dublin, 2001–	
European Causeway	2000	410	375	Larne–Cairnryan, 2000–	
European Gateway	1975	326		Larne–Cairnryan, 1980–1982	
European Highlander	2002	410	375	Larne–Cairnryan, 2002 -	
Express Olbia	1966	1600	386	Cork–Pembroke Dock, 1980	
Felicity	1980	1600	517	Fishguard–Rosslare, 1990	
Fennia	1966	1200	255	Cork–Pembroke Dock, 1983	
Free Enterprise I	1962	1400	120	Larne–Cairnryan, 1975	
Free Enterprise III	1966	1200	221	Larne–Cairnryan, 1974	
Free Enterprise IV	1969	1200	280	Larne–Cairnryan, 1976–1986	
Galloway Princess	1980	974	309	Stranraer–Larne, 1980–1990	
Goelo	1967	1170	210	Roscoff–Cork, 1981	

Name	Built	Passengers	Cars	Irish Sea Routes	Notes
Gotland	1973	1670	300	Rosslare–Le Havre/Cherbourg, 1988	
Hampton Ferry	1934	800	40 trucks + 25 cars	Stranraer–Larne, 1953–1961	
Havelet	1977	550	205	Roscoff–Cork, 1992	ex-*Cornouailles*
Hengist	1972	1400	217	Fishguard–Rosslare, 1985	
Holyhead Ferry 1	1965	1000	153	Holyhead–Dun Laoghaire, 1965–1973, Stranraer–Larne, 1966/66/67, Heysham–Dun Laoghaire, 1970/71, Fishguard–Rosslare, 1973	
Horsa	1972	1400	217	Holyhead–Dun Laoghaire, 1990, Fishguard–Rosslare, 1990	
Hoverspeed Boulogne	1991	450	85	Stranraer–Belfast, 1993	
Hoverspeed Great Britain	1990	450	85	Stranraer–Belfast, 1993, Belfast–Heysham, 2001, Belfast–Douglas, 1993.	
Innisfallen (IV)	1969	1149	280	Cork–Swansea, 1969–1979, Dublin–Liverpool, 1979–1980	
Innisfallen (V)	1969	1380	280	Cork–Pembroke Dock, 1980–1983, Rosslare–Pembroke Dock, 1983–1986, Dublin–Holyhead, 1986, Rosslare–Fishguard, 1986	ex-*Leinster (V)*
Ionian Sun	1969	1380	280	Cork–Swansea, 1990	ex-*Innisfallen (V), Leinster (V)*
Ionic Ferry (I)	1958			Larne–Cairnryan, 1973	
Ionic Ferry (II)	1967	1300	350	Larne–Cairnryan, 1986–1992	ex-*Dragon*
Isle of Inishmore (I)	1981	1500	386	Dublin–Holyhead, 1992–1993/94/95, Rosslare–Pembroke, 1993–1996	ex-*Leinster (VI)*
Isle of Inishmore (II)	1997	2200	856	Dublin–Holyhead, 1997–2001, Rosslare–Pembroke Dock, 2001–	
Isle of Inishturk	1981	1500	386	Rosslare–Pembroke Dock, 1996–1997	ex-*Isle of Inishmore (I)*
Isle of Innisfree (I)	1986	2000	411	Rosslare–Pembroke Dock, 1991–1993/94–95, Dublin–Holyhead, 1993–1994	
Isle of Innisfree (II)	1995	1650	600	Dublin–Holyhead, 1995–1997/98/99/2000, Rosslare–Pembroke Dock, 1997–2001	
Jetliner	1996	600	160	Larne–Cairnryan, 1996–2000	
Jonathan Swift	1999	800	200	Dublin–Holyhead, 1999–	
King Orry	1975	1000	220	Douglas–Heysham/Liverpool/Dublin/Dun Laoghaire, 1990–1998 Liverpool–Dublin, 1998	ex-*Channel Entente, Saint Eloi*

Name	Built	Passengers	Cars	Irish Sea Routes	Notes
Koningin Beatrix	1986	2100	500	Pembroke Dock–Rosslare, 1997, Fishguard–Rosslare, 1997–2002, Dublin–Holyhead, 1999, Cork–Roscoff, 1998	
Lady of Mann	1976	800	130	Douglas–Liverpool & seasonal routes, 1976–, Dublin–Fleetwood, 1996, Liverpool–Dublin, 1997.	Capacity figures post 2001 refit
Lagan Viking	1997	340	130 trailers + 100 cars	Belfast–Liverpool, 1997 -	
Leinster (V)	1969	1380	280	Dublin–Liverpool, 1969–1980, Cork–Swansea, winter relief	
Leinster (VI)	1981	1500	386	Dublin–Liverpool, 1981–1998, Dublin -Holyhead, 1982–1992, Rosslare–Pembroke Dock, 1984	
Leopard	1968	850	250	Le Havre–Rosslare, 1968/69/70/71	
Lion	1967	1200	160	Belfast–Ardrossan, 1968–1975	
Lord Warden	1952	1000	120	Holyhead–Dun Laoghaire, 1971/73/79, Fishguard–Rosslare, 1978, Fishguard–Dun Laoghaire, 1978	
Maid of Kent	1959	1000	180	Holyhead–Dun Laoghaire, 1979, Stranraer–Larne, 1975, Fishguard–Rosslare, 1976	
Manx Maid	1962	1400	70	Douglas–Liverpool & seasonal routes, 1962–1984.	
Manx Viking	1976	777	125	Douglas–Heysham, 1978–1986	
Mersey Viking	1997	340	130 trailers + 100 cars	Belfast–Liverpool, 1997–date	
Mona's Isle	1966	1200	220	Douglas–Heysham/Dun Laoghaire, 1985	ex-*Free Enterprise III*
Mona's Queen	1972	1200	100	Douglas–Liverpool & seasonal routes, 1972–1990, Holyhead–Dun Laoghaire, 1988	
Munster (V)	1968	1000	220	Dublin–Liverpool, 1968–1981/82/83, Rosslare–Pembroke Dock, 1981–1983	
Munster (VI)	1970	1040	238	Rosslare–Pembroke Dock, 1990–1992, Dublin–Holyhead, 1990/91	
Normandy	1981	2100	700	Rosslare–Roscoff/Cherbourg, 1998–date, Rosslare–Pembroke Dock, relief 1998–date	
Normannia	1952	500	111	Holyhead–Dun Laoghaire, 1965	

Name	Built	Passengers	Cars	Irish Sea Routes	Notes
Norröna	1973	1040	250	Rosslare–Pembroke Dock, 1989–1990, Dublin–Holyhead, 1990, Holyhead–Dun Laoghaire, 1994, Fishguard–Rosslare–1994, Stranraer–Larne, 1995	
Norse Lagan	1967	200	140 trailers + 50 cars	Belfast–Liverpool, 1991–1997	
Penn-ar-Bed	1974	250	235	Roscoff–Cork, 1978/81	
Pioneer	1974	356	60	Douglas–Heysham, 1993	
Pont-Aven	2004	2400	650	Roscoff–Cork, 2004–	
Pride of Ailsa	1972	610	370	Larne–Cairnryan, 1992–1996	
Pride of Rathlin	1973	610	370	Larne–Cairnryan, 1992–2000	
Prince of Brittany	1970	1020	210	Roscoff–Cork, 1979 Rosslare–Le Havre/Cherbourg, 1981	
Prinsessan Desirée	1971	1400	250	Rosslare–Pembroke Dock, 1981, Holyhead–Dun Laoghaire, 1981	
Prins Hamlet	1973	1100	275	Rosslare–Pembroke Dock, 1988	
Prins Philippe	1973	1302	243	Rosslare–Fishguard, 1986	
Quiberon	1975	1402	260	Roscoff–Cork, 1982–1989	
Rapide	1996	677	160	Liverpool–Dublin/Douglas, 2001 Belfast–Heysham, 2002, Belfast–Troon, 2003–date	
Saint Colum I	1973	1090	230	Belfast–Liverpool, 1982–1990, Rosslare–Fishguard, 1987	ex-*Saint Patrick*
Saint Eloi	1975	1000	220	Stranraer–Larne, 1989, Holyhead–Dun Laoghaire, 1989	
Saint Killian	1973	1500	320	Rosslare–Le Havre/Cherbourg, 1978–1982.	
Saint Killian II	1973	2000	418	Rosslare–France, 1982–1997, Dublin–Liverpool/Holyhead, 1994	ex-*Saint Killian*
Saint Patrick	1973	1090	230	Rosslare–Le Havre/Cherbourg, 1973–1982. Rosslare–Pembroke Dock, 1981	
Saint Patrick II	1973	1500	420	Rosslare–France, 1982–1997 Relief roles on Dublin–Holyhead and Rosslare–Pembroke Dock	
Scottish Coast	1957	1400	25	Belfast–Ardrossan, 1965–1968 Belfast –Liverpool, 1968	
Seacat Danmark	1991	427	85	Stranraer–Belfast, 1998, Douglas–Liverpool & seasonal routes, 1998, Belfast–Heysham, 1999	ex-*Hoverspeed Boulogne*
SeaCat Isle of Man	1991	477	85	Douglas–Liverpool & seasonal routes, 1994–1995, 1997, 1999–date. Relief roles on Belfast–Stranraer/Troon.	

Name	Built	Passengers	Cars	Irish Sea Routes	Notes
SeaCat Scotland	1992	427	85	Stranraer–Belfast 1992–2000. Belfast–Troon, 1999–2002.	
Senlac	1973	1400	217	Rosslare–Fishguard, 1987.	
Shepperton Ferry	1934	800	40 trucks + 25 cars	Stranraer–Larne, 1962/63/64/65.	
St Anselm	1980	1200	309	Fishguard–Rosslare, 1983.	
St Brendan	1974	1400	420	Fishguard–Rosslare, 1985–1990.	ex-*Stena Normandica*
St Christopher	1981	1000	309	Holyhead–Dun Laoghaire, 1981. Fishguard–Rosslare, 1981.	
St Columba	1977	2400	335	Holyhead–Dun Laoghaire, 1977–1990. Fishguard–Rosslare, 1982	
St David (III)	1947	1300	73	Fishguard–Rosslare, 1964–1969, Holyhead–Dun Laoghaire, 1969, Heysham–Dun Laoghaire, 1970	
St David (IV)	1981	1000	309	Holyhead–Dun Laoghaire, 1981–1985/86/87/88, Stranraer–Larne, 1983/84/85, 1986 1991. Fishguard–Rosslare, 1983–1988, relief.	
Stena Adventurer	1977	1700	335	Holyhead–Dun Laoghaire, 1996, Stranraer–Belfast, 1996	ex-*Stena Hibernia, St Columba*
Stena Adventurer (II)	2003	1500		Holyhead–Dublin, 2003–date	
Stena Antrim	1981	1370	309	Stranraer–Larne, 1991–1995, Holyhead–Dun Laoghaire, 1995, Fishguard–Rosslare, 1995, Stranraer–Belfast, 1995–1996	ex-*St Christopher*
Stena Caledonia	1981	1000	309	Stranraer–Larne, 1991–1995, Stranraer–Belfast, 1995–date, Fishguard–Rosslare, 1998, Rosslare–Roscoff, 1998	ex-*St David (IV)*
Stena Cambria	1980	1300	309	Holyhead–Dun Laoghaire, 1991–1996/97, Holyhead–Dublin, 1998, Fishguard–Rosslare, 1990/91/92/93, Stranraer–Larne, 1992/95	ex-*St Anselm*
Stena Challenger	1991	500	480	Holyhead–Dublin, 1996–2001, Cork–Roscoff, 1998	
Stena Discovery	1997	1500	350	Stranraer–Belfast, 1997	
Stena Europe	1981	1800	405	Fishguard–Rosslare, 2002–	
Stena Explorer	1996	1500	350	Holyhead–Dun Laoghaire, 1996–date, Stranraer–Belfast, overhaul relief. 2000–date	
Stena Felicity	1980	1600	517	Fishguard–Rosslare–1990–1997	ex-*Felicity*
Stena Forwarder	2001	1000		Holyhead–Dublin, 2001–2003	

Name	Built	Passengers	Cars	Irish Sea Routes	Notes
Stena Galloway	1980	974	309	Stranraer–Larne, 1990–1995, Stranraer–Belfast, 1995–2002, Holyhead–Dun Laoghaire, 1992, Fishguard–Rosslare, 2001	ex-*Galloway Princess*
Stena Germanica	1967	1300	220	Cork–Swansea, 1978	
Stena Hengist	1972	1400	256	Holyhead–Dun Laoghaire, 1992, Stranraer–Larne, 1992	ex-*Hengist*
Stena Hibernia	1977	1700	335	Holyhead–Dun Laoghaire, 1991–1996	ex-*St Columba*
Stena Horsa	1972	1400	256	Holyhead–Dun Laoghaire, 1992.	ex-*Horsa*
Stena Invicta	1985	1720	350	Holyhead–Dublin, 1999–2000, Fishguard–Rosslare, 2000	
Stena Londoner	1974	1800	425	Fishguard–Rosslare, 1996, Holyhead–Dun Laoghaire, 1996	
Stena Lynx	1993	427	85	Stranraer–Belfast, 1998, Holyhead–Dun Laoghaire, 1996, Fishguard–Rosslare, 1996–1998	ex-*Stena Sea Lynx*
Stena Lynx III	1996	650	160	Holyhead–Dun Laoghaire, 1999, Stranraer–Belfast, 1999, Fishguard–Rosslare, 1999–	
Stena Nordica (I)	1965	965	135	Stranraer–Larne, 1966–1971, Belfast–Ardrossan, 1970	
Stena Nordica (II)	1975	1200	450	Fishguard–Rosslare, 1980, Rosslare–Pembroke Dock, 1980–1981	
Stena Normandica	1974	1200	420	Fishguard–Rosslare, 1979–1985	
Stena Sea Lynx	1993	427	85	Holyhead–Dun Laoghaire, 1993–1994, Fishguard–Rosslare, 1994	
Stena Sea Lynx II	1994	600	145	Holyhead–Dun Laoghaire, 1994–1995	
Stena Voyager	1996	1500	350	Stranraer–Belfast, 1996, Holyhead–Dun Laoghaire, 1997	
Superferry	1972	1400	330	Cork–Swansea, 1993–2000, 2002–date	
SuperSeaCat Three	1999	700	150	Liverpool–Dublin, 1999–2000 Douglas–Liverpool, 2000	
SuperSeaCat Two	1997	680	150	Liverpool–Dublin, 1998 Belfast–Heysham–2000, Liverpool–Dublin/Douglas, 2003–date	
SuperStar Express	1997	600	175	Larne–Cairnryan, 2000–date	
The Viking	1974	1200	330	Dublin–Holyhead, 1989	
Tregastel	1971	1500	370	Roscoff–Cork, 1985	
Tynwald	1967	1200	155	Douglas–Heysham/Dun Laoghaire, 1986–1990.	ex-*Antrim Princess*
Ulster Prince	1968	1008	140	Belfast–Liverpool, 1967–1981	
Ulster Queen	1968	1008	140	Belfast–Liverpool, 1967–1981	

Name	Built	Passengers	Cars	Irish Sea Routes	Notes
Ulysses	2001	1875	1342	Dublin–Holyhead, 2001–date Dublin–Liverpool, 2002	
Val de Loire	1987	2280	600	Roscoff–Cork, 1993–2003	
Venus	1976	878	350	Cork–St Malo, 1999	
Viking III	1964	940	180	Douglas–Heysham, 1980, Rosslare–Pembroke Dock, 1980	
Viking Victory	1964	940	180	Douglas–Heysham, 1981	
Villandry	1965	1380	160	Stranraer–Larne, 1982, Douglas–Heysham, 1983, Holyhead–Dun Laoghaire, 1983	
Vortigern	1969	1000	240	Fishguard–Rosslare, 1987	

The largest fast ferries on the Irish Sea are Stena Line's HSS ships *Stena Explorer* and *Stena Voyager*. The regular vessel on the Belfast–Stranraer route is the *Stena Voyager*, seen here running astern on to the linkspan at Belfast on 12 October 2002. *Norman Johnston*

Index to photographs

Acknowledgements

First and foremost my wife Phil is thanked for her unwavering support while her husband disappeared into a relationship with his computer. Big hugs to Ian, Simon, AJ and Jenna for leaving Daddy in peace and most of all for sacrificing their computer games time!

The Masters, Officers and Crews of Sealink UK's Holyhead ships and in particular 'The Railway Children', are warmly thanked for their friendship and encouragement during my childhood years.

Richard Danielson, well known for his beautifully written books on Isle of Man Steam Packet favourites is thanked for his time and assistance in the selection of many photographs of vessels in his area.

Grateful thanks are also extended to the following for their warm and most welcome assistance with this work; Jim Ashby, Stan Basnett, Bettina Bomford, Paddy Cahill, John Cave (Holyhead Maritime Museum), Brian Cleare, Ian Collard, Philip Coombs, Gary Davies (Maritime Photographic), Capt Roy Graves, Capt Tudor Jones, Capt Richard Jones, Trevor Kidd (Larne Ferryweb), Capt Neville Lester, Aiden McCabe (Irish Ships.com), Capt Wyn Parry (Stena Line), Jack Phelan, Richard Seville, Adrian Sweeney (Ships of Mann), Ian Scott-Taylor, Nigel Thorntonn, Rob de Visser and Barry Watts.

Justin Merrigan
Western Australia
November 2004

If you enjoyed reading this book, then these Colourpoint publications may also be of interest.

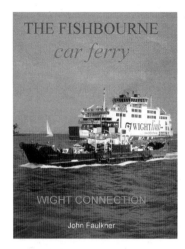

The Fishbourne Car Ferry
Wight Connection
John Faulkner

1 904242 30 8 £16
160pp, pbk,
260 x 210mm,
120 b/w and colour
photos.

15 March 1926 saw the opening of a new six mile car ferry service between Portsmouth and the tiny village of Fishbourne on the Isle of Wight. This book looks at the history of the Fishbourne car ferry and speculates on what may lie ahead. It is intended to be of general interest as well as providing something for shipping enthusiasts and local historians. Also included is some interesting technical data on the ships along with recollections of men who worked them.

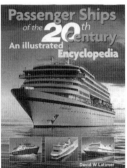

Passenger Ships of the 20th Century
An Illustrated Encyclopedia
David Latimer

1 898392 70 6 £50 hbk,
400pp 280 x 210 mm,
over 450 photos

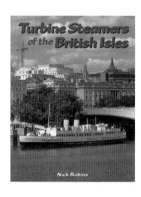

Turbine Steamers of the British Isles
Nick Robins

1 898392 38 2 £11.99
125pp, 232 x 180 mm,
73 b/w photos.

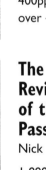

The Decline and Revival of the British Passenger Fleet
Nick Robins

1 898392 69 2 £14.99
160pp, 232 x 180 mm,
134 b/w photos

Death in the North Channel
The loss of the Princess Victoria, January 1953
Stephen Cameron

1 904242 01 4 £13.99
144pp, 260 x 210mm
167 b/w photos.

View the full range of Colourpoint titles at our web site: www.colourpoint.co.uk